Pipes, Mains, Cables and Sewers

Sixth Edition

H W Wilkinson, LLM, PhD

Solicitor
Department of Professional Legal Studies
University of Bristol

FT

LAW & TAX

© Pearson Professional Limited 1995

H W Wilkinson has asserted his right under the Copyright,
Designs and Patents Act 1988 to be identified as the author of
this work

ISBN 075200 1906

First Edition 1967
Sixth Edition 1995

Published by
FT Law & Tax
21–27 Lamb's Conduit Street
London WC1N 3NJ

A Division of Pearson Professional Limited

Associated Offices
Australia, Belgium, Canada, Hong Kong, Luxembourg,
Singapore, Spain, USA

No responsibility for loss occasioned to any person acting or
refraining from action as a result of material in this publication
can be accepted by the authors or the publishers.

A CIP catalogue record for this book is available
from the British Library.

Printed and bound in Great Britain by
Hartnolls Limited, Bodmin, Cornwall

Contents

Preface

In the past decade there has been increasing emphasis on environmental concerns, not only in this country but also in Europe and worldwide. Many of the legal provisions relating to water, sewage and waste disposal have been consolidated and re-enacted. The courts have been active also. This edition has been substantially re-structured and amended to reflect the changed emphasis.

The law is stated as at 13 March 1995 but the chapters on water, sewers and land drainage should be read subject to the Environment Act 1995, on which a separate chapter is included.

It has been assumed that the Environment Bill, the Channel Tunnel Rail Link Bill and the Gas Bill, all of 1995, have been enacted in the general form set out in the Bills.

H W Wilkinson
Department of Professional Legal Studies
University of Bristol
March 1995

Table of Cases

Table of Statutes

Table of Statutory Instruments

Part I

Laying by Private Agreement, Implication or Prescription

Chapter 1

The Necessary Characteristics of a Pipe Easement

In *Re Ellenborough Park* [1956] Ch 131, at 163, the Court of Appeal accepted that the essential requirements of a valid easement at common law are set out in *Cheshire's Modern Law of Real Property* (now *Cheshire and Burn's Modern Law of Real Property*, 15th ed (Butterworths 1994), pp 520–4). These requirements are:

(1) There must be a dominant and a servient tenement.
(2) The easement must accommodate the dominant tenement.
(3) The dominant and servient owners must be different persons.
(4) The right must be capable of forming the subject-matter of a grant.

The characteristics are fully treated in *Gale on Easements*, 15th ed (Sweet & Maxwell 1986), pp 6–30 and P Jackson, *The Law of Easements and Profits* (Butterworths 1978), pp 5–21. Only those aspects which particularly concern pipes will be discussed here. It will be convenient to follow the order of classification already given.

1 Dominant and servient tenements

To constitute an easement in private law there must be a dominant tenement to which the right belongs and a servient tenement upon which the obligation is imposed (*Mounsey v Ismay* (1865) 3 H & C 486, per Martin B, at 497). There can be no easement in gross (see (1980) 96 LQR 557, M F Sturley, criticising the weak theoretical basis of the rule).

Where there is an express grant the two tenements must be defined by the deed creating the easement, or be capable of definition through evidence of the circumstances surrounding

3

the transaction: *Johnstone v Holdway* [1963] 1 QB 601 (CA) (identification of the dominant tenement by evidence of material facts at the date of execution when the deed failed to identify); *The Shannon Ltd v Venner Ltd* [1965] Ch 682 (CA) (evidence of the intentions of the purchaser when the deed was made was admitted to help to construe words used in the deed); *Bracewell v Appleby* [1975] Ch 408 (the fact that a right of way was over a private road serving private houses was relevant in construing a grant over the road of 'a right of way of the fullest description'); *White v Richards* (1994) 68 P & CR 105 (CA) (extent of a way expressly reserved to be ascertained from words of reservation and surrounding circumstances).

Where the grant is by prescription or implication, evidence of the extent of the user enjoyed over the statutory period or of the circumstances of the implication will delineate the tenements. A person claiming a pipe easement will usually be able to point out what land is burdened by tracing the route of the pipe, and the land benefited should be apparent from the place where the pipe terminates on his land and the function it fulfils.

The dominant tenement is usually corporeal property, a plot of land or a building served by a cable or pipe. In *Bass v Gregory* (1890) 25 QBD 481, the dominant tenement was an underground cellar used for brewing and the owner was held to have an easement for a current of air to come along to it through a ventilation tunnel under the servient tenement.

There is some authority for saying that an easement, which is incorporeal, can be appendant to incorporeal property—a right attached to a right. In *Hanbury v Jenkins* [1901] 2 Ch 401, a person claimed a right to a fishery over part of the River Usk and a right of way along both banks for angling purposes. He established his incorporeal right to a fishery, the servient tenements being the banks over which the right of way ran. *AG v Emerson* [1891] AC 649 was quoted by Buckley J (at 411), as establishing that the owner of the fishery is presumed, in the absence of contrary evidence, to own the soil of the river bed and this is the dominant tenement, but he added that, even if this were not so and the right to the fishery were incorporeal only, the incorporeal right of way could be appendant to it if there was agreement between the rights 'in nature and quality so as to be capable of union without any incongruity' (at 422). This reasoning could be used to claim for the owner of a pipe the right to go onto the land over which it runs to inspect and repair it, but the objection that the presumption concerning the ownership of the bed of a river does not apply to the soil supporting a pipe is a cogent one. A sounder argument to justify such an entry on land is that the grant of an easement carries with it all ancillary easements necessary for its exercise and enjoyment (*Bulstrode v Lambert* [1953] 1 WLR 1064), and this would include reasonable inspection and repair.

Dominant tenement

The dominant tenement may comprise both corporeal hereditaments (land and buildings) and incorporeal hereditaments (rights over land). In *Re Salvin's Indenture* [1938] 2 All ER 498 a water company had a right by deed to lay water pipes through a person's land. The question arose whether this was an easement or merely a personal licence and therefore unenforceable against any but the parties to the original deed. The water company owned no land contiguous to the burdened land, so the landowner contended that this was a claim to an easement in gross, as there was no dominant tenement. Farwell J held that there was a valid easement, the dominant tenement being the water undertaking itself, consisting of corporeal hereditaments (lands owned by the company for the purpose of its objects) and incorporeal hereditaments (the rights acquired in the lands of others, such as to lay pipes).

In view of this decision the practitioner may feel justified in advising a client that the combination of a landholding connected in some way, however remote, by pipes to the servient land and a right granted to lay his pipes there, will constitute a dominant tenement sufficient to support a claim to an easement.

The unfortunate aspect of the case is that it is difficult to imagine any circumstances in which it would be held that there was no grant of easement in a similar situation unless the parties expressly agreed and stipulated against a grant. Possibly the judge was impressed by the consequences of holding that the water company's widespread system of pipes was laid under personal licence only. *Hanbury v Jenkins* [1901] 2 Ch 401 does not seem to have been cited in *Re Salvin*. It is suggested that the doctrine of non-derogation from grant could have been properly used in *Re Salvin* to prevent the successor in title to the grantor from obstructing the water company's rights (*Cable v Bryant* [1908] 1 Ch 259, per Neville J, at 264). It was held in *London & Blenheim Estates Ltd v Ladbrooke Retail Parks Ltd* [1993] 4 All ER 157 (CA) that a right to nominate additional, at present unspecified, land as the dominant tenement to the servient land could not create an interest which would bind successors in title to the servient land, followed in *Voice v Bell* [1993] EGCS 128 (CA).

Servient tenement

The servient tenement will always be corporeal property, a plot of land or a building burdened in some way by the right of the dominant owner. In many cases, although it is clear which is the servient land, it is not clear how much of it is to be regarded as burdened. For example, if the servient land is a five-acre field over one strip of which a pipe runs by virtue of an easement, can the dominant owner claim that because he has an easement the servient owner could not sell off, say, four acres over which the pipe does not run, free of all burden? Either the vendor who sells off land should stipulate that the part is sold subject to the easement 'if and so far as' it affects the plot (which is rather vague conveyancing) or the purchaser should satisfy himself that it does not affect the plot and take a conveyance free from it, if necessary by getting the dominant owner to join in and release any possible right over the part sold off.

In most cases the easement will only burden materially that part of the land over which the pipe runs to a sufficient width and extent to ensure access to it to the dominant owner for the purpose of inspection and repair and to a sufficient depth and width to afford support to the pipe (*Newcastle-under-Lyme Corporation v Wolstanton Ltd* [1947] Ch 427). So the dominant owner can restrain a use of the servient land which will prevent him from enjoying his easement or make enjoyment substantially more difficult than previously. In *Goodhart v Hyett* (1884) 25 ChD 182, the court restrained the servient owner from building over the line of a pipe which served the dominant land because the exercise of the right of the dominant owner to inspect and repair the pipe after the building was erected would have involved him in substantially more work and expense than if there were no building there.

The whole of the five-acre field mentioned in the example is burdened in the sense that the existence of the easement upon it may prevent its being sold as a complete unit as readily as if there were no easement. A plot of land subject to a right of way cannot be as easily sold as a site for a factory or department store as if the right did not exist. The Law Reform Committee (14th Report,

Cmnd 3100 (1966)) suggested that the Lands Tribunal should have power to discharge an easement or substitute one easement for another (para 97) but no legislation has resulted.

2 Easement must accommodate dominant tenement

In *Re Ellenborough Park* [1956] Ch 131, per Evershed MR, at 170, it was said that a right claimed over the land of another cannot be an easement unless it accommodates and serves the dominant tenement and is reasonably necessary for the better enjoyment of it; the right must have a necessary connection with the dominant tenement. In *Hill v Tupper* (1863) 2 H & C 121, the plaintiff leased land adjoining a canal, with the exclusive rights of running pleasure boats on it. The defendant, who had an inn on the canal, also let out boats on it. The plaintiff sued for interference with his 'easement'. He failed, the court saying that his claim was unconnected with his use and enjoyment of his demised land. Pipes will readily be seen to accommodate the premises they serve. The supply of water and the carrying away of effluent are reasonably necessary for the better enjoyment of premises. In *Wong v Beaumont Property Trust Ltd* [1965] 1 QB 173 (CA), a claim to affix a ventilation duct for kitchens onto adjoining premises was held to be an easement; in this case the duct was necessary for the enjoyment and continued use of the premises, under local authority requirements.

It is quite common to find older-type adjoining houses sharing chimneys and chimney stacks, with their flues leading into the same chimney. In this case there will usually be mutual easements of user and support and mutual obligations of repair. The mutual easements are reasonably necessary for the enjoyment of both premises (*Jones v Prichard* [1908] 1 Ch 630).

Cases could be envisaged where the right claimed does not accommodate the dominant tenement, for example, a claim to water one's cattle from a pipe on nearby private land. In *Re Ellenborough Park*, above, it was said that a right to a seat at Lord's cricket ground or to visit the zoo could not be an easement annexed to the ownership of a private dwelling-house, there being no sufficient nexus between the right and the enjoyment of the ownership (Evershed MR, at 174). It was held in *Rance v Elvin* (1983) 49 P & CR 65 that where water was supplied to plot *A* through a meter on plot *B* the owner of plot *A* could not claim an easement to have the water come to his land. The supply depended upon the owner of plot *B* being willing to continue to take the water and pay the charges. To impose a positive obligation on him to go on doing so would breach the principle that save in the anomalous case of an easement of fencing (*Lawrence v Jenkins* (1873) LR 8 QB 274) a right in the nature of an easement can only impose a negative obligation on the servient owner. Even though the claimed dominant owner was willing to pay his share of the charges for the water, he could not impose an easement where none was possible. It was further held on appeal in *Rance v Elvin* (1985) 50 P & CR 9 (CA) that though the owner of plot *B* had no obligation to ensure that water came through the pipes the owner of plot *A* had an easement for the passage of any water which did come through. For the distinction between a right to a supply of water and a right to the passage of water see *Schwann v Cotton* [1919] 2 Ch 459 (CA).

3 Dominant and servient owners

The dominant and servient owners must be different persons. Anyone who, for example, lays an electricity cable across his own land is not granting himself an easement but is exercising an incident of ownership (*Metropolitan Railway Co v Fowler* [1892] 1 QB 165, per Lord Esher MR, at 171).

Can one person, however, in one capacity, acquire an easement for himself in another capacity, so that it continues when he disposes of the servient land? This question was raised, though not conclusively answered, in *Ecclesiastical Commissioners for England v Kino* (1880) 14 ChD 213, where the question was whether windows of a church could acquire a right to light by prescription over the glebe lands adjoining. Both were vested in the rector, the church in him as trustee, the glebe lands in him as beneficial owner. An interlocutory injunction was granted to restrain building and all three members of the Court of Appeal indicated their view that the rector as beneficial owner could have burdened the glebe lands with a right to light for windows of the church of which he was trustee. But presumably in the converse situation, if the rector as trustee sought to burden the trust land for the benefit of the glebe land, he would be restrained from a dealing to his own advantage (*ex p Lacey* (1802) 6 Ves 625).

Other possible double relationships exist: sole personal representative against sole beneficiary, family company against husband and wife who are sole shareholders. Despite the obiter dicta in *Kino's* case, it is suggested that the practitioner cannot safely advise that a person can acquire easements for or against one or other of his legal personalities in this way. The rule in *Wheeldon v Burrows* (1879) 12 ChD 31 should be borne in mind and if the 'double personality' owner sells off part of the land he should expressly reserve over the land sold any rights which he wishes to continue to enjoy as easements. A person without capacity cannot grant an easement expressly or impliedly. In the case of *Re St Clement's, Leigh-on-Sea* [1988] 1 WLR 720 it was held that the incumbent of a church had no power to grant impliedly an easement over the churchyard; a faculty of an ecclesiastical court was needed.

A tenant cannot acquire by prescription an easement over land of his landlord not demised to him, because the occupation of the tenant is in law the occupation of the landlord (*Gayford v Moffat* (1868) 4 Ch App 133, per Lord Cairns LC at 135). The exception is that a tenant can prescribe for an easement of light, Prescription Act 1832, s 3.

A limited company is a legal person (*Salomon v Salomon & Co Ltd* [1897] AC 22). Company mergers and amalgamations may affect easements; if *A* Co Ltd has a right to run a pipe over the adjoining land of *B* Co Ltd and the companies merge the easement will be extinguished by unity of seisin (*Whalley v Tompson* (1799) 1 Bos & P 371, per Eyre CJ, at 375). The easement will not revive for the benefit again of the amalgamated company if the land of the former *B* Co Ltd is sold off. It should be expressly reserved afresh for the benefit of the retained land (*Wheeldon v Burrows* above).

Where there is more than one dominant owner enjoying an easement over the servient land, one of them cannot sue the other for causing physical damage to the subject of the easement by excessive user unless the damage is such as substantially to interfere with and obstruct the plaintiff's own enjoyment of the easement (*Weston v Lawrence Weaver Ltd* [1961] 1 QB 402).

4 Right must be capable of forming subject-matter of grant

The following considerations are important in this connection:
(1) Are the rights expressed in terms too wide and vague?
(2) Would they amount to joint occupation with the servient

owner or substantially deprive him of proprietorship or legal possession?

(3) Do they possess qualities of utility and benefit (*Re Ellenborough Park* [1956] Ch 131, per Evershed MR)?

Furthermore, just as the intending grantor must be capable of granting (*Mulliner v Midland Railway Co* (1879) 11 ChD 611), so the proposed grantee must be capable of taking a grant. A grant cannot be made to a company with no power to hold easements (*National Guaranteed Manure Co v Donald* (1859) 4 H & N 8). Nor can there be a grant to an uncertain and fluctuating body such as the electorate of Birmingham, although in an old decision, *Gateward's Case* (1607) 6 Co Rep 59 *b*, the inhabitants of a town established an 'easement' of way by custom over land. This would nowadays be called a public right of way and not an easement. A person with an interest in land cannot grant an easement over it in excess of his interest; he cannot grant an easement in fee simple over land on which he has a 99 year lease, and the grant will take effect for the residue of his term. If he subsequently acquires the reversion, this will not enlarge the easement (*Booth v Alcock* (1873) 8 Ch App 663). Similarly, a grantee cannot acquire an easement if it would be greater than his own interest in the land benefited (*Wheaton v Maple & Co* [1892] 3 Ch 48).

Vagueness

A claim will not be allowed if it cannot be defined. For example, a right of air to premises can be acquired over the land of another provided that the air flows in a defined channel, such as down a passage or tunnel (*Chastey v Ackland* [1895] 2 Ch 389), or provided that the air flows to definite windows or apertures on the dominant premises (*Hall v Lichfield Brewery Co* (1879–80) 49 LJ Ch 655). Only the former type of right concerns pipe easements as it constitutes in effect a right to have a 'pipe' (tunnel or channel) maintained on someone else's land. In *Chastey v Ackland*, above, Lopes J said (397) that a claim must be shown to have the air pass through some definite channel constructed for the purpose of containing and communicating it. This is too narrow a proposition and a right could be acquired for air down a roofed-in passage between two buildings, or down a narrow passage not roofed in between tall buildings (sometimes called a 'ginnel' in Lancashire and a 'snickelway' in Yorkshire) even if they were not originally constructed for the purpose of communicating the air.

There can, of course, be no claim to an easement for air which passes at large over another's land (*Webb v Bird* (1861) 10 CB (NS) 268). Such a claim is too vague and the servient owner would have no means of obstructing it and thus of preventing the acquisition of an easement (*Harris v De Pinna* (1886) 33 ChD 238, per Bowen LJ, at 262). But such a right could be claimed under the doctrine of non-derogation from grant (*Lyme Valley Squash Club Ltd v Newcastle-under-Lyme Borough Council* [1985] 2 All ER 405).

There can be an easement which is only enjoyed occasionally. From *Penn v Wilkins* (1974) 236 EG 203 it appears that a right could be recognised to lay temporary pipes through a neighbour's land to the dominant owner's cess-pit and to pump out the effluent to a tanker standing in the road, whenever the cess-pit needed emptying. The claim under s 62 of the Law of Property Act 1925 failed, because the 'right' was not enjoyed when the purchaser bought, the cess-pit being constructed after purchase.

If water percolates underground in an undefined channel no one can claim an easement to have it come to him through his neighbour's land; the claim is too vague. His neighbour could lawfully collect and use it, even if the effect were to stop the percolating supply, *Acton v Blundell* (1843) 12 M & W 324, or to cause the collapse of his land, *Stephens v Anglian Water Authority* [1987] 1 WLR 1381 (CA). The rule is otherwise if the water flows in a defined underground channel; here a claim against an abstracting neighbour will lie (*Chasemore v Richards* (1859) 7 HL Cas 376). This is a less usual type of pipe easement, not a claim to use and send water along an underground course on someone else's land, but to have water come along the course to one's land and to prevent the neighbour from abstracting the flow or polluting it (*Stockport Waterworks Co v Potter* (1864) 3 H & C 300). It includes in many cases also the more usual right to pass the water on along someone else's land.

Joint occupation

A person who makes such a wide claim to use land that in effect he demands the full beneficial ownership will not succeed in establishing that he has an easement over it (*Copeland v Greenhalf* [1952] Ch 488; unsuccessful claim to station and repair unspecified number of vehicles on neighbour's land). But temporary exclusion of the servient owner is a feature of many easements, for example, when a kitchen is shared (*Heywood v Mallalieu* (1883) 25 ChD 357) or when there is shared use of a lavatory in an office (*Miller v Emcer Products Ltd* [1956] Ch 304). In contrast, in *Wright v Macadam* [1949] 2 KB 744, a right to use a coal shed, apparently virtually excluding the owner, was accepted as a right passing under Law of Property Act 1925, s 62. Unless the servient owner himself connects into and uses the pipe of the dominant owner on his land the dominant owner will have exclusive use of the part of the servient land occupied by his pipe. This will not bring him into conflict with *Copeland v Greenhalf* since he does not claim, in effect, beneficial ownership of the servient land as a whole, nor does he substantially deprive the servient owner of proprietorship or legal possession. In many cases the existence of a pipe through land will have no restrictive effect at all on the use to which it can be put; crops can be grown over it if it is well buried and cattle can graze over it. If the pipe does interfere with the surface use, the question to what degree the servient owner is ousted from his enjoyment becomes important; relevant considerations are the amount of the exclusion (for example, the size of the pipe in relation to the area of the land), the permanence or otherwise of the exclusion and the length of time it continues or is likely to continue.

Utility and benefit

It would be unusual to find a case of a claim to a pipe easement which was not of utility and benefit to the dominant tenement. Even a claim to run a pipe over someone else's land to convey water to an ornamental fountain on one's own land would probably be upheld. The right to use a part as a pleasure garden was held in *Re Ellenborough Park* [1956] Ch 131 to be a right of utility and benefit and a beneficial attribute of residence in an adjoining dwelling-house. In this case some doubt was expressed by the court (177–9) whether the alleged distinction between a right of utility and benefit on the one hand and 'mere recreation and amusement' has any justifiable basis in law (it has its origin partly in the case of *Mounsey v Ismay* (1865) 3 H & C 486). The categorisation must be a false one, for recreation is a benefit and amusement is of utility. This requirement is probably inoperative in the sense that the alleged easement will not be held invalid under this head alone; if it fails it will do so under one of the other heads also—vagueness, joint ownership or being ultra vires.

It was stated by the court in *Re Ellenborough Park*, above, that the categories of easement are not closed and in that case a new easement was recognised but because the law has developed fully over many years it is unlikely that many more will be found. In *Phipps v Pears* [1965] 1 QB 76 (CA) it was held that there was no easement for protection from the weather by one building for another, followed in *Marchant v Capital and Counties Property Co Ltd* (1982) 263 EG 661 (but reversed on other grounds on the interpretation of an award under the London Building (Amendment) Act 1939 at (1983) 267 EG 843 (CA)). There may be a benefit for protection from the weather derived incidentally if one building has an easement of support from another (*Bradburn v Lindsay* [1983] 2 All ER 408).

Chapter 2

The Nature of the Right to Lay and Use Pipes

1 As an easement

Some conflict of view has existed on whether the right to lay a pipe in another's land is an easement or not.

The right to the exclusive use of a water pipe running through adjoining land was recognised as an easement in *Goodhart v Hyett* (1884) 25 ChD 182, per North J, at 186; in *Nuttall v Bracewell* (1866) LR 2 Ex 1, per Martin B, at 10, it was said that the right to a flow of water in a goit is a well-known easement.

On the other hand it was held in *Bevan v London Portland Cement Co Ltd* (1892) 67 LT 615 that a person who had constructed and enjoyed the exclusive use of a tunnel under land adjoining his own land had gained a good title to the tunnel itself by limitation and that the enjoyment was not a mere easement. And in *Metropolitan Railway Co v Fowler* [1893] AC 416 it was held that for rating purposes the right to make a tunnel was the grant of a hereditament and not an easement. A case similarly decided concerning the right of drainage through a watercourse is *Holywell Union v Halkyn Drainage Co* [1895] AC 117. But the issue here was not between dominant and servient owners but between the taxpayer and the Revenue.

The majority of easements are of two kinds; they are either a right to do something on someone else's land, such as to go across it on a defined track (*Cannon v Villars* (1878) 8 ChD 415), or a right to prevent him from doing something on his land which will affect his neighbour's land, such as building so as to restrict light (*Colls v Home & Colonial Stores Ltd* [1904] AC 179) or excavating so as to remove support (*Dalton v Angus* (1880–1) 6 App Cas 740). In these cases, although the servient owner is limited in his use of his land, he is not excluded from any of his land. The pipe

14

easement is different. It consists of the right to put something in or on someone else's land, to maintain it there and to use it there, for example, by passing liquids along it. The right to tunnel involves in addition removing part of the neighbour's land and passing through the cavity thus made. These pipe easements in effect exclude the owner from the part of his land which is occupied by the pipe or tunnel. Now as a general rule a grant of the exclusive use of a piece of land takes effect as a grant of the land itself for all the estate therein of the grantor (*Reilly v Booth* (1890) 44 ChD 12). The courts will not uphold a claim to an alleged easement which in effect amounts to a claim to exercise the rights of full ownership (*Copeland v Greenhalf* [1952] Ch 488). But in view of the other rights already recognised as easements which involve exclusion of the owner permanently from part of his land, for example, a right to construct a yard on another's property and store goods there (*Mast v Goodson* (1772) 3 Wils 348), and a right to project a timber staging over adjoining land (*Harris v De Pinna* (1886) 33 ChD 238), the general rule cannot be an absolute one. There is, as has been indicated, weighty judicial authority for saying that the right to lay pipes in land and use them exclusively is an easement. Support is provided by *South Eastern Railway Co v Associated Portland Cement Manufacturers* (1900) *Ltd* [1910] 1 Ch 12, at 27; and in *Dunn v Blackdown Properties Ltd* [1961] Ch 433 the matter was treated as self-evident.

A validly created easement, held for the equivalent of a term of years absolute or of a fee simple absolute in possession, is a legal interest (Law of Property Act 1925, s 1(2)(*a*)). In *Land Reclamation Co Ltd v Basildon District Council* [1979] 1 WLR 106 (*affirmed* at (1979) 38 P & CR 528 (CA)) a local authority validly granted under seal a right of way for a term of just under seven years. An easement for a term other than these takes effect as an equitable interest (Law of Property Act 1925, s 1(3)). A legal easement is valid even against a bona fide purchaser for value of the servient land without notice of it. An equitable easement will bind such a purchaser only if protected by registration as a land charge, Class D (iii) (Land Charges Act 1972, s 2), and in the case of land with a registered title, as a minor interest (Land Registration Act 1925, ss 3(*xv*), 49(1)). For an example of a right in the nature of an equitable easement, but arising out of mutual benefit and burden and not registrable as a land charge, see *E R Ives Investments Ltd v High* [1967] 2 QB 379 (CA).

Under the Law of Property Act 1969 the statutory period of a good root of title in contracts made after the Act took effect (1 January 1970) is 15 years (s 23). The purchaser of land may thus not have actual knowledge of a land charge (such as an equitable easement) registered after 1925 but before his root of title commences. He is none the less bound by the land charge but if he suffers loss by reason of its existence he is entitled to compensation from the Chief Land Registrar (s 25). If he had actual knowledge he can have no compensation, but by s 24(1) registration of the land charge under the Land Charges Act 1925 or the Land Charges Act 1972 (1972 Act, s 18(5)), is not deemed to constitute actual knowledge, despite s 198 of the Law of Property Act 1925.

There can be different rights in different segments of the same land, as where a person has mining rights under the land of another. In *Williams v Usherwood* (1983) 45 P & CR 235 (CA) it was held that a person who lost his title to land by reason of the adverse possession of it by his neighbour nonetheless retained a right to go upon it to maintain his property and to drain his house through it. See also *Marshall v Taylor* [1895] 1 Ch 641 (CA).

The word 'easement' has been loosely used by the courts and Parliament. It has been applied to rights which may or may not have the characteristics of common law easements. For example, a landowner whose land was severed by a railway gained an easement to pass over it to reach his land on the other side, under the Railways Clauses Consolidation Act 1845, and this might well have the characteristics of a common law easement. On the other hand, under s 7 of the Coastal Flooding (Emergency Provisions) Act 1953, a person may have a right to use a private road or 'formed way' to perform works of sea defence even if he owns no land to be benefited, and this will not have the characteristics. These 'statutory easements' will be so called in this book. The article of that name by Professor J F Garner in (1956) *The Conveyancer*, 20, at 208, is very helpful. The precise use of terminology may help by reminding the practitioner that, in cases where rights over another's land are granted by private agreement (or implied or prescribed for), he must ensure that the easement is a valid one at common law, but that where the grant is by authority of statute the wording of the enabling Act is paramount. In *Mulliner v Midland Railway Co* (1879) 11 ChD 611, the company, which had compulsorily acquired land under an Act, was held on the construction of the Act to have no right under it to go on to grant an easement over the land. In *Central Electricity Generating Board v Jennaway* [1959] 3 All ER 409, it was held that where the

Electricity (Supply) Act 1919, s 22, granted the Board a right to pass overhead wires over land it conferred also by implication the right to the ancillary easement of erecting and maintaining on the land pylons to support them.

2 Under a licence

Types of licence

If a licence to enter on someone else's land is granted without payment or other consideration (a bare licence), the grantor can revoke it at will on reasonable notice without being liable in damages. In *Armstrong v Sheppard & Short Ltd* [1959] 2 QB 384 a person allowed another to lay a drain in his land and later gave about five weeks' notice to the grantee of revocation of the permission. This notice was held sufficient.

If a licence is granted for money or money's worth one party cannot terminate it otherwise than in accordance with the contract, provided that the other party is behaving properly and in accordance with the agreement (*Hurst v Picture Theatres Ltd* [1915] 1 KB 1). One might have a case where a market gardener pays for a licence from a neighbouring landowner to run temporary water pipes over the neighbour's land to serve some outlying fields during the season from 1 April to 15 September. If on 1 July the neighbour revokes the licence, so that the crops in the fields are ruined, the market gardener can claim damages for breach of contract. The *Encyclopaedia of Forms and Precedents* (the *Encyclopaedia*), 5th ed (Butterworths) Vol 12, 1269–70, and *Precedents for the Conveyancer* (Sweet & Maxwell), vol 1, 3034 give precedents.

Difficulty may be found in distinguishing between a grant of easement and of licence. In *IDC Group Ltd v Clark* [1992] 2 EGLR 184 (CA) 'Licence' was granted by deed to pass through a doorway over the grantors' land in case of fire and to use corridors and passages to the public street. By one clause the terms 'grantors' and 'grantees' included their respective successors and assigns. A successor refused access, claiming that she was not bound by the 'Licence'. It was held that, the deed having been drafted professionally, the phrase 'grant Licence' must be taken to have been used with the intention of creating a licence and not an easement. Successors were not bound.

A licence may be coupled with a proprietary interest in the land of the licensor, for example, a licence to go on the land to cut grass and take it away. Rights to use pipes would rarely involve taking anything away from the land. If they did, such as a right to lay a pipe and extract brine through it, they would be profits à prendre and should be created by deed or prescription to be enforceable against a third party (Law of Property Act 1925, ss 1(2), 52(1)). A contract for grant of a profit à prendre must be in writing signed by or on behalf of each party; where contracts are exchanged each part must comply (Law of Property (Miscellaneous Provisions) Act 1989, s 2). If the interest is equitable it must be protected as a land charge under s 2(4) of the Land Charges Act 1972, or by notice in the case of registered land, if it is to bind a third party.

If a licensor has led the licensee to change his position (such as by spending money on his premises) in the expectation that the licence will be permanent, the licensor will be estopped from revoking the licence (*Dillwyn v Llewelyn* (1862) 4 De GF & J 517; *Inwards v Baker* [1965] 2 QB 29). In *Ward v Kirkland* [1967] Ch 194 a verbal permission to lay and use drains was held in the circumstances to be permanent and unlimited in time, as it would have been unconscionable for the grantor to revoke his permission when expenditure had been made in reliance on it, but in *Armstrong v Sheppard & Short Ltd* [1959] 2 QB 384 a verbal right to use a drain was held revocable on reasonable notice, although the grantor could not require the grantee to remove the drain which he had allowed to be laid in his land. If the adjoining landowners have granted each other mutual benefits, such as a right of way, of drainage or of allowing the encroachment of foundations, one of them will not be allowed to enjoy the benefit of the arrangement whilst rejecting the burden. He may not withdraw the licence unilaterally: *Hopgood v Brown* [1955] 1 WLR 213 (CA) (mutual drainage rights); *E R Ives Investments Ltd v High* [1967] 2 QB 379 (CA) (right of way and use of foundations).

Position of third parties

If the licensor sells his land, can the licensee enforce the licence against the purchaser? The grant of a licence is in general a transaction personal to the parties so that even a person who takes the land with notice of the licence is not bound by it. In *King v David Allen & Sons, Billposting Ltd* [1916] 2 AC 54 a licence to post bills on a cinema wall was held unenforceable by the licensee against the successor in title of the licensor, who had taken the premises with notice of the licence: *Midland Bank Ltd v Farmpride Hatcheries Ltd* (1980) 260 EG 493 (CA) should be contrasted. Equity has intervened in certain situations to make licences enforceable by and against successors in title of licensors and licensees. Some of the cases have been mentioned above. For example, where there is an expenditure of money in the expectation (induced by the licensor) that the licence will be permanent, the successor in title with notice is bound by it (*Inwards v Baker*, above); similarly where there are mutual licences granted by adjoining landowners (*E R Ives Investments Ltd v High*, above).

Equity may regard the purchaser who takes with notice of a licence as being subject to a constructive trust. In *Binions v Evans* [1972] Ch 359 (CA) a purchaser of premises bought them expressly subject to the right of an elderly lady to live in them for her lifetime rent-free. The purchaser was held not to be entitled to revoke her right and to turn her out, though he had made no contract or agreement with her. He was a constructive trustee of the premises to the extent of her interest in them.

It was the view of Lord Denning in *Bendall v McWhirter* [1952] 2 QB 466 (and in *Binions v Evans*, above) that even against a purchaser for value a contractual licensee who is in actual occupation of land by virtue of a licence has an interest which is valid, if not at law then in equity, against the successors in title of the licensor so long as the conditions of the licence are observed. It is not a legal interest in the land but a clog or fetter like a lien. The occupation by the licensee is sufficient notice of his rights to a purchaser (Law of Property Act 1925, s 14; Land Registration Act 1925, s 70(1)(*g*)). The doctrine has not found favour with the House of Lords (*National Provincial Bank Ltd v Ainsworth* [1965] AC 1175, at 1239, 1251). In contrast, Megarry and Wade, *The Law of Real Property*, 5th ed (Stevens 1984) p 808, changing its opinion from the 4th ed (1975) p 783, says 'all the indications now are that contractual licences are capable of binding successors in title as equitable interests (or perhaps as mere equities)'. Cheshire and Burn's *Modern Real Property*, 15th ed (Butterworths 1994) p 592, says after a review of the cases (and citing in support dicta in *Ashburn Anstalt v Arnold* (1987) 2 EGLR 71 (CA)) that they 'provide no support for the view that contractual licences generally are binding on third parties. However, *Emmet on Title*, 19th ed, (FT Law & Tax) para 5.156 says unconvincingly, 'It has been at least arguable (although perhaps heretical) that a person having a licence to use land may hold an equitable licence enforceable against a purchaser other than one who takes a legal estate for value without notice'. It was held in *Midland Bank Ltd v Farmpride Hatcheries Ltd* (1980) 260 EG 493 (CA) that a licence can bind third parties (there a mortgagee) who have merely constructive notice and not actual notice.

In *Cook v Minion* (1978) 37 P & CR 58 *A*'s predecessor in title permitted *B*'s predecessor in title to re-lay his drains so as to run through *A*'s drain. *A* was held bound to continue to allow *B* to do the same, since *B*'s predecessor had incurred expense in reliance on the permission.

Is a licence registrable under the Land Charges Act 1972? Section 2 of the Act authorises registration under Class D (iii) as an equitable easement of any easement, right or privilege created or arising after 1925 and being merely an equitable interest. In *E R Ives Investments Ltd v High*, above, the Court of Appeal seems to have held that a mutual licence (of way for the one party and of support of foundations for the other) was not registrable, and in *Shiloh Spinners Ltd v Harding* [1973] AC 691 the House of Lords held that an equitable right of re-entry on breach of covenant was not registrable. Perhaps Class D (iii) is confined to equitable easements and rights in the nature of easements and profits. If a licence has the support of a dominant tenement to be benefited by it, it is suggested that it is registrable under Class D (iii). Where the title to the land is a registered one, then if the licensee has drainage rights or water rights or is in possession he may be held to have an overriding interest which is not capable of entry on the register but subject to which all dispositions will take effect (Land Registration Act 1925, s 70(1)). Section 70(1) gives (amongst others) as overriding interests 'drainage rights, . . . watercourses, rights of water, and other easements not being equitable easements required to be protected by notice on the register' (para (a)) and 'the rights of every person in actual occupation of the land . . ., save where enquiry is made of such person and the rights are not disclosed' (para (g)). If he is not in possession and does not possess water rights he will not have an overriding interest. Any other type of licence over registered land seems not to be an overriding interest, and it is not clear whether it is registrable against the land as a minor interest under ss 3(xv) and 49(1) of the Land Registration Act 1925. Ruoff and Roper on *The Law and Practice of Registered Conveyancing*, (Sweet & Maxwell 1991) para 8.02, say that in unregistered land licences arising by estoppel are not registrable as land charges, but in registered land they can be protected by notice, restriction or caution, Land Registration Act 1925, ss 49(1)(f), (2), 53 and 54.

Can the licence be assigned to a person who buys the licensee's land? A bare licence is personal to the grantee and will cease on an assignment (*Terunnanse v Terunnanse* [1968] AC 1086). A licence protected by equity can be enjoyed and enforced by the successor in title of the licensee (*Hopgood v Brown* [1955] 1 WLR 213). A licence coupled with an interest in land is assignable (*Muskett v Hill* (1839) 5 Bing NC 694, at 707–8 (licence to mine for and remove tin ore)). A contractual licence is not assignable unless the contract so provides (*Clore v Theatrical Properties Ltd* [1936] 3 All ER 483).

The case of *Re Salvin's Indenture* [1938] 2 All ER 498 (discussed in the previous chapter) is a very important one. If ever it is held to have been wrongly decided, many pipes now thought to be laid by virtue of easements may be found to be laid by virtue of personal licences. Problems of enforcement by and against successors in title would then become acute.

3 Under the doctrine of non-derogation from grant

The doctrine that a grantor may not derogate from his grant has been applied in certain cases to enforce obligations which could not ordinarily be protected as easements. A person entitled to an easement of light cannot object to any and every diminution made in his light by his neighbour, but in *Herz v Union Bank of London* (1854) 2 Giff 686, a person who took a lease of premises for the express purpose of carrying on his business of a diamond merchant and who needed a greater amount of light to his windows than most businesses would need was able to restrain his lessor from diminishing the light which he enjoyed and required. An example concerning pipes (in this case, a ventilation duct) is provided by *Wong v Beaumont Property Trust Ltd* [1965] 1 QB 173 (CA), where an assignee of a lessee restaurant-owner was held to be entitled to affix a duct from his kitchens to a wall of the assignee of the landlord on premises not included in the lease to comply with the requirements of the public health authority. The court found here an easement of necessity, but the grounds of the decision have been criticised by the writer (inter alios), who has suggested that the doctrine of non-derogation is a more appropriate ground ((1964) *Modern Law Review*, 27, 720). It is appreciated, however, that this suggestion involves an extension of the doctrine: from restraining a person who has made a grant from doing something more which will derogate from it, to not permitting him to derogate by *failing* to do something—for example, to give his permission for a ventilation duct to be affixed to his wall. It is suggested that derogation can just as much occur by not doing, as by doing.

The doctrine can be applied against an assignee of the grantor's interest whether or not he is aware of the obligation (*Cable v Bryant* [1908] 1 Ch 259, per Neville J, at 264). So if a landowner sells off part of his land for the known purpose that a house can be built on the part sold, and the house is built with drains lawfully running through the part retained and the landowner sells the land retained to a person who commences excavations which will damage the drains, this person can be restrained under the doctrine from so doing.

Can an assignee of the grantee's interest invoke the doctrine against the grantor or the grantor's successor in title? This point is open. *Wong's* case, above, supports the view that he can. Further, since it has been decided that the obligation binding the grantor is enforceable against his successors (*Cable v Bryant*, above), then the successors of the grantee should acquire his rights so long as they use the premises for the same purpose as gave rise to the original benefit in the grantee. *Gale on Easements*, 15th ed, p 103, supports the view, but gives *Harmer's* case (below) as an authority, which does not support it. *Cook v Minion* (1978) 37 P & CR 58 now supports it.

The doctrine is not limited to physical interference with the enjoyment of the land demised; non-physical interference is included. Where a lessee took land for an explosive store and adjoining land was leased by the same lessor to a person who built so near to the store that the licence to store explosives was revoked by the Home Office, it was held that by the subsequent leasing the lessor had derogated from his first grant (*Harmer v Jumbil (Nigeria) Tin Areas Ltd* [1921] 1 Ch 200). This decision could be of importance where the first grant is of a right to lay a pipe carrying a dangerous or corrosive substance and a subsequent grant is made which may turn this into a more hazardous matter than previously, such as a grant of a plot of land on which fuel tanks are to be erected.

It will be unusual to find pipes laid affected by the doctrine or to find them laid by licence. They are far more likely to be laid by virtue of an easement. Accordingly, subsequent discussion will largely concern itself with pipe easements, though the observations may be relevant to the other types of case.

The doctrine of non-derogation from grant is discussed in (1964) *Law Quarterly Review*, 80, 244 (D W Elliott).

4 Trespass

A person who connects his drain to someone else's without permission and uses it is liable for trespass even if the other suffers no damage. However, an injunction will not necessarily be granted to restrain the trespass. In *Cook v Minion* (1978) 37 P & CR 58 a person without permission connected the drainage of his house to a common pipe which served several houses. An injunction was refused since it would be oppressive to the defendant if he were ordered to alter the drainage arrangements of his house. Damages were awarded instead.

5 Common law rights of drainage

Where land is on the bank of a watercourse (whether the water flows on or below ground) the proprietor or occupier of the land is entitled to the flow and bound to accept it. He is not entitled to deprive landowners lower down of the flow, nor to pen it back on the land of his upstream neighbour, *Mason v Hill* (1833) 5 B & Ad 1, 110 ER 692.

Where land is not on the bank of a watercourse:

(a) where water does not run in a defined channel but runs freely over the surface or percolates through the soil a higher owner may appropriate the water (for example, in a reservoir) no matter how long the lower owner has enjoyed it, *Broadbent v Ramsbotham* (1856) 11 Ex 602, 156 ER 971;

(b) the lower owner cannot complain of water coming from the higher land but is not bound to accept it and can put up barriers to it, even if this causes damage to the higher land, *Home Brewery Co Ltd v William Davis & Co (Leicester) Ltd* [1987] 2 WLR 117;

(c) the owner of land has no right to discharge, such as by pumping, water onto his neighbour's land which has come there by gravity, *Baird v Williamson* (1863) 15 CB (NS) 145, or which has come naturally but has been kept there artificially, *Whalley v Lancashire and Yorkshire Railway Co* (1884) 13 QBD 131, and is liable if he has collected it there and it escapes, *Rylands v Fletcher* (1868) LR 3 HL 330;

(d) an occupier may protect his land from floodwater, by sea or river, and build defences against it even if the result is that it flows with greater violence onto someone else's land but he may not injure his neighbour's land in getting rid of the water (see *Whalley's case* above).

Chapter 3

Acquisition of the Pipe Easement and Extent of the Right

1 Acquisition by deed or other express grant

A landowner's power to grant easements of whatever nature he chooses over his land is subject to certain restrictions.

First, planning permission will be required if the work to be carried out constitutes 'development'. The Town and Country Planning Act 1990, s 55(1), defines development as 'the carrying out of building, engineering, mining or other operations in, on, over or under land, or the making of any material change in the use of any buildings or other land'. Section 55(2) lists certain matters which do not constitute development, including the carrying out of works by a local authority or statutory undertaker for 'inspecting, repairing or renewing any sewers, mains, pipes, cables or other apparatus' (para (c)). This does not exempt such work by private persons and it does not include the laying of new services. By s 55(2) of the Act, the carrying out of works for alteration of a building by providing additional space therein below ground does constitute development, despite the general rule in s 55(2) that alterations to the interior which do not materially affect the external appearance are not development. Certain works of development may be 'permitted development' under the Town and Country Planning General Development Order 1988 (SI No 1813), in which case there is no need to obtain an express grant of planning permission before carrying them out unless the land is in an area of special control such as a National Park.

The permitted developments are given in Sched 2 of the 1988 Order and include:

(a) the enlargement, improvement or other alteration of a dwellinghouse up to stated sizes (Pt 1);

(b) development on industrial land including the provision or re-arrangement of a sewer, main, pipe, cable or other apparatus (Pt 8, Class B);

(c) carrying out works for inspecting, repairing, or renewing any sewer, main, pipe, cable or other apparatus (Pt 10, Class A);

(d) development authorised under any local or private Act for erecting or altering any bridge, aqueduct, pier or dam (Pt 11, Class A);

(e) development by water authorities and for sewerage and sewage disposal (Pts 15 and 16);

(f) other parts authorise developments for providing or replacing sewers, drains or cables by water or hydraulic power undertakings (Pt 17, Class C); gas suppliers (Pt 17, Class F); electricity undertakings (Class G); tramway or road transport undertakings (Class H); mining operations (Pt 19, Class A); British Coal mining development (Pt 20); and telecommunications development (Pts 24 and 25).

A second restriction on the freedom to grant easements is that the landowner may not grant a right which is contrary to the public good, such as a right to drain into and pollute a stream contrary to public health regulations. In the case of water rights he cannot grant a right which will prejudice owners of other sections of the watercourse, unless they consent. Draining heated water into a river and so killing the fish is an example (*Pride of Derby & Derbyshire Angling Association Ltd v British Celanese Ltd* [1953] Ch 149).

A third requirement is the obvious one that the easement sought to be granted must have the characteristics of a common law easement discussed in the previous chapter.

Creation of easement

It is essential to the grant of a legal easement that it is created by deed (Law of Property Act 1925, s 52(1)). If so made it is enforceable against all persons taking any interest in the servient land. It is not registrable under the Land Charges Act 1972. The only exception to the requirement for a deed is where the easement is granted or reserved under a disposition by will; a legal easement will arise when the assent is made by the personal representatives but will relate back to the date of death (Administration of Estates Act 1925, s 36(2), (4)). A contract to grant a legal easement must be in writing, signed by or on behalf of each party (Law of Property (Miscellaneous Provisions) Act 1989, s 2). A grant made otherwise than by deed will take effect as an equitable easement which will depend on registration under the Land Charges Act 1972, s 2, under Class D (iii) for enforceability against persons acquiring a legal estate in the servient land for money or money's worth (s 4(6); Land Registration Act 1925, s 52(1)). In *Huckvale v Aegean Hotels Ltd* (1989) 58 P & CR 163 (CA) it was held that where a person was granted an easement of way by contract but failed to protect it by registration, the right did not bind the purchaser of the servient tenement. Where the grantee has bound himself to buy land to be benefited by a grant of easement but has not at the date of the grant taken a conveyance, assignment or (in the case of registered title) transfer, it is suggested that the grant becomes completely effective and the legal easement arises when the conveyance or assignment is made, and in the case of a transfer when the transfer is registered at the Land Registry (Land Registration Act 1925, ss 20(1), 22(1)). Until then the grant takes effect in equity only (*Johnstone v Holdway* [1963] 1 QB 601 (CA)) but if the title is a registered one and the right is actually enjoyed it may take effect as an overriding interest, *Celsteel Ltd v Alton House Holdings Ltd* [1985] 2 All ER 562.

An order for specific performance may be made against a person who covenants to make sewers under his own land for the benefit of land which he has sold off for building and who fails to make them: in *Carpenters Estates Ltd v Davies* [1940] Ch 160 it was held that in such a situation, where the plaintiff could not reasonably build until the defendant had carried out his covenant to make the sewers which would serve the buildings, damages would not be an adequate remedy.

Construction of grant

It is a rule of construction of a grant of water easements, laid down by Jessel M R, in *Taylor v St Helens Corporation* (1877) 6 ChD 264, at 270–1, that one must find out the meaning of the instrument according to the ordinary and proper rules of construction and that the maxim that in cases of doubt or obscurity the grant must be read against the grantor is of no force. In this case he pointed out that the grant of a watercourse, particularly when coupled with other words, might mean the easement for the running of water, the drain which carries the water or the land over which the water flows. He said that if the context did not show which was meant then the easement for the running of water was meant. Where water rights over land are created under a deed the nature and extent of the interests of the parties is regulated wholly by the deed, and the court cannot consider what rights they would have had as riparian owners if they had not made the deed (*Northam v Hurley* (1853) 1 E & B 665); the rule applies also to underground water in springs (*Whitehead v Parks* (1858) 2 H & N 870).

Where the meaning of the deed is clear, evidence cannot be given that it means something other than what it appears to mean, for that would be to contradict the deed. Only if the deed is not plain may the court consider the circumstances surrounding the making of the grant (*The Shannon Ltd v Venner Ltd* [1965] Ch 682, per Danckwerts LJ, at 693). The court's task is to ascertain the parties' intentions by construing the deed, and it will consider (*a*) the circumstances surrounding the execution of the instrument, and (*b*) whether there have been words inserted limiting the type of user (*Cannon v Villars* (1878) 8 ChD 415, per Jessel MR, at 420–1). In *Shayler v Woolf* [1946] Ch 320 (CA) the defendant conveyed a plot of land adjoining his own to Mrs Peacock for the erection of a bungalow and he covenanted to supply water to the premises from a pump on his own land and to keep the pump in good repair and working order. Mrs Peacock sold the bungalow to the plaintiff Mr Woolf, with the benefit of the covenant. The pump became blocked and a new one was made nearby but the defendant refused to continue the supply to the plaintiff, who then claimed specific performance. It was held that on the true construction of the agreement it was the intention of the parties that the benefit of the covenant should be assignable, otherwise it would cease on the death of the grantor, and the bungalow would at once be much reduced in value. The argument that the supply of water was one for personal services which equity would not enforce was rejected by the court, as was the argument that the duty to maintain the pump should not be enforced as it would involve the covenantor in renewing the pump completely from time to time. The court said that repair need not necessarily involve renewal.

In *St Edmundsbury and Ipswich Diocesan Board of Finance v Clark (No 2)* [1975] WLR 468 (CA) it was held that a reservation of a 'right of way' was ambiguous and must be construed by looking at the surrounding circumstances at the time of the grant. Here the path of the way appeared not to be a roadway but a derelict and overgrown path when the grant was made and therefore it was a way for passage on foot, not a vehicular way. Although a reservation was, by s 65(1) of the Law of Property Act 1925, technically a re-grant by the purchaser the question of whether there was any presumption either as against the vendor or the purchaser only fell to be considered when the court was unable on the material before it to reach a sure conclusion on the proper construction of the reservation. A purchaser can create an easement over the property which he is buying, by having it conveyed to him 'subject to' the easement which is to be created (1925 Act, s 65(2)); an unidentifiable person can take an interest in land even though he is not a party to the conveyance, 1925 Act, s 56, *Wiles v Banks* (1985) 50 P & Cr 80.

Drawing the grant

Identifying tenements

Although it is desirable to identify the dominant tenement which the easement will benefit, the grant will not be ineffective if this is not done, provided the court can satisfy itself by evidence of the material facts existing when the deed was made what was the whole object of the transaction (*Thorpe v Brumfitt* (1872–3) 8 Ch App 650). As a matter of prudent drafting, however, the dominant tenement should certainly be identified, as should the servient tenement (*Woodman v Pwllbach Colliery Co Ltd* [1915] AC 634). It is suggested that the same rules are applicable to ascertain the servient tenement as to ascertain the dominant tenement.

In *Land Reclamation Co Ltd v Basildon District Council* [1979] 1 WLR 106 (affirmed at (1979) 38 P & CR 528) where a right of way was granted for a term of years, by deed, Brightman J said that it was well established that a right of way could exist as a legal interest notwithstanding that the dominant tenement was not precisely identified in the deed of grant: 'The general purpose reference to the company's land in the lease is sufficient for this purpose, extrinsic evidence being admissible' (p 110).

It is proper conveyancing practice not only to identify the dominant land but also the owners or occupiers of it so as to make it doubly clear what land is benefited (Danckwerts LJ in *The Shannon Ltd v Venner Ltd* [1965] Ch 682, at 692). *Kelly's Draftsman*, 16th ed, contains a useful precedent.

The dominant and servient plots should be indicated on a plan unless they can safely and completely be identified otherwise, by street numbers for example. The line of the pipe should be indicated so that the places of its beginning and end are clear. For a declaration as to party walls and drains where part of land is sold off see *Kelly's Draftsman*, 16th ed.

If an easement is granted to serve dominant tenement *A*, can the same easement be used to accommodate dominant tenement *B* which the easement owner later acquires? The need for tight drafting is shown here. The common law position was set out by Romer LJ in *Harris v Flower* (1904) 74 LJ Ch 127, where he said that if a right is granted for the enjoyment of plot *A* and the grantee owns or acquires plot *B* he cannot use the way to plot *A* to accommodate plot *B* also. The principle would apply where a right to lay a pipe to plot *A* was granted and plot *B* was sought to be connected onto the pipe. In *Bracewell v Appleby* [1975] Ch 408 a person was granted a right of way 'of the fullest description' over a private road to gain access to his plot (number 3) in a cul-de-sac. Six plot owners shared the private way to reach their plots in the cul-de-sac. The owner of plot 3 bought some land-locked land which was behind it (plot 2a) and made a way to plot 2a over his plot 3, and thence over the way in the cul-de-sac, despite protests from other plot owners. The additional use was held not to be permitted by the grant and damages were awarded. An injunction to forbid use was refused, as it would have made the house on plot 2a unusable. The correctness of the decision to refuse an injunction in *Bracewell* was strongly doubted by Scott J in *Anchor Brewhouse Developments Ltd v Berkley House (Docklands Developments) Ltd* [1987] 2 EGLR 173.

Purpose and extent

The purpose and extent of the grant should be stated. For example, in *Land Reclamation Co Ltd v Basildon District Council* [1979] 1 WLR 106 a right of way was validly granted by deed for a company between stated times to pass along a private road 'for all purposes in connection with the use of the Company's land for the dumping and disposal of waste materials'. If a pipe is to drain away rainwater the servient owner should stipulate this so that it is not subsequently adapted to be used for sewerage or other polluted water. If only a general description is given, such as 'for the purpose of drainage of the dominant premises', then the pipe can be used for any purpose which it will accommodate (*White v Grand Hotel Eastbourne Ltd* [1913] 1 Ch 113; *Keefe v*

Amor [1965] 1 QB 334 (CA)). But even though a grant is in wide terms a particular use could be forbidden if to allow it would restrict the use which could be made by others who also have a right to use the land: *Jelbert v Davis* [1968] 1 WLR 589 (CA) (grant of right to use a way 'in common with all others having the like right'; proposal to put 200 caravans on adjoining land, with their occupiers using the way; held: not permissible for these numbers to use the way, their use would interfere with those 'having the like right').

In *Rosling v Pinnegar* (1987) 54 P & CR 124 (CA) a person bought a large house which had a right of way to be used 'in common with the purchaser and all persons deriving under him'. He restored the house with a grant from public funds which required him to open it to the public on not less than 30 days in the year. The right of way was originally granted 'for all purposes'. It was held that the mere attraction of visitors along the way was not itself a breach of the terms of the easement but since on the facts user had been such as to interfere unreasonably with use by others who were entitled to the way an injunction would issue to control and limit the use.

If the servient owner wishes to limit the intensity of user he should stipulate this also; the dominant owner might build other premises on his land and seek to drain these through the same pipe, and the result might be overloading of the pipe with danger of fracture or overflow, as in *Wood v Saunders* (1875) 10 Ch App 582. Unless he stipulates that the pipe is to serve the particular dominant premises existing at the date of the grant, the servient owner may have difficulty in preventing increased intensity of user. Relevant questions are whether the grant was a limited one or a general one, and whether the use complained of goes outside the terms of the grant (*Hurt v Bowmer* [1937] 1 All ER 797). In *Phillimore v Watford Rural District Council* [1913] 2 Ch 434 a person with a right to drain water over someone else's land was restrained from draining sewage over it. It was held in *Coopind (UK) Ltd v Walton Commercial Group Ltd* [1989] 1 EGLR 241 that lessees of premises on an industrial estate under a lease which granted them the right to receive a supply of (inter alios) gas to the premises, could require the lessors to permit the laying of a gas main on the lessors' land to bring a fivefold increase in the gas supply. The nature of the tenants' activities in making industrial gas turbines and developing new types, the length of the lease (20 years), and the absence of any burden on the lessors to handle the supply, were all relevant considerations.

Care should be taken to state precisely the extent of the grant. Where a right is to be granted to drain foul water into a sewer for example, it is of little use to grant a right to pollute 'to the extent and in the manner and with the materials at present being discharged' if it has not been established what this manner, extent and materials consist of. Some means should be found of making an agreed measure or description which should then be contained in the grant itself or incorporated into it by reference, for example, 20,000 gallons per day, or between the hours of 10 pm and 6 am. For a precedent which allows drains which may be made in the future (within the perpetuity period) to be connected, see *Precedents for the Conveyancer*, vol 2, 8099. In *Trailfinders v Razuki* (1988) 2 EGLR 46 it was held that a lease which reserved to the landlords the free passage of electric current from other buildings of the landlords through the wires and conduits 'which are now or hereafter during the term' may be in, over or under the demised premises, did not entitle the landlords to lay and use new cable for a computer link-up to their adjoining premises. For a precedent for laying computer cables see *Precedents for the Conveyance*, vol 2, prec 19.55, p 9678, Eric Dumbill.

It is not possible to give fixed meanings to certain standard conveyancer's phrases; the meaning will differ with the situation. For example, in *Collins v Slade* (1874) 23 WR 199, a grant of a right of way 'as at present enjoyed' was held to mean that user was restricted to certain daylight hours. In *Hurt v Bowmer*, above, the phrase in a grant of a way over a field 'as at present enjoyed' was held to have no relevance to the purpose for which the way was used at the time of the grant but only to the quality of user—whether on foot or with vehicles. Since the plaintiff's complaint was over the quantity of user since the grant and not over its quality and type, which had remained the same, he was unsuccessful.

In *Polden v Bastard* (1865) LR 1 QB 156, a person owned two adjoining houses. She occupied one and let the other to a tenant, Thomas Answood, who used the water pump which was on her premises as he had no water supply. The owner devised her own house to the plaintiff and the other 'as now in the occupation of Thomas Answood' to her niece, who later conveyed it to the defendant. The plaintiff refused access to the pump on his property and the defendant took water by forcible entry. It was held that he was not entitled to water from the pump. The devise had merely identified the property being conveyed; it had not evinced an intention to pass an easement to the devisee of the tenanted property. In this case there was no easement of necessity as the tenant could have sunk a well on his premises or have used a nearby river.

Where the right is given to a class of persons (such as to *A*, his heirs, assignees, tenants and licensees) it is a question of construction of the grant whether the list is exhaustive or illustrative (*Hammond v Prentice Bros Ltd* [1920] 1 Ch 201).

The grant of a particular type of easement may by implication put an obligation on the grantor. In *Liverpool Corporation v Irwin* [1977] AC 239, at 256–7, Lord Wilberforce suggested that if a right to use a passage was granted and the natural light was absent or insufficient 'to the extent that the easement is useless without some artificial light being provided, the grant should carry with it an obligation to take reasonable care to maintain adequate light'. This is a novel suggestion. The general rule is that the only easement which can impose a duty to expend money is the 'spurious easement' of fencing (*Lawrence v Jenkins* (1873) LR 8 QB 274). P Jackson, *The Law of Easements and Profits*, at 65 considers that Lord Wilberforce's suggestion could be better put upon the basis of non-derogation from grant.

Contents of deed

Normal provisions in a deed of grant are arrangements for laying, inspecting, cleansing and repairing the pipes (a right of entry will be granted to the dominant owner for this purpose), and for paying for the cost of laying the pipes and legal and surveyor's fees in connection with drawing the deed and obtaining any necessary consents. The deed should stipulate that the plans and specifications of the pipes are to be approved by the grantor before construction commences and that the works should comply with the plans. There should be a right to inspect them at various stages before they are covered, and laying should not proceed beyond each stage until approved. Construction should comply with the Building Regulations 1991 (SI No 2768) and the current British Standard Code of Practice. It may be thought wise to have a sum to cover the cost of the works deposited in a bank account in the joint names of the solicitors for the grantor and the grantee and a right to the grantor to use the moneys to have the laying completed should the grantee fail to do so within a specified time after due notice to complete. This will cover the contingency of the grantee going bankrupt. A precedent for the grant of an easement to lay a pipe and to drain through it into a septic tank is contained in the *Encyclopaedia*, 5th ed, vol 12, p 1269; for general grants and reservations of rights of drainage in registered land see Ruoff and West, *Land Registration Forms* 3rd ed, (Sweet & Maxwell 1983) pp 75, 76, 130, 131, 141, 142.

Further matters to consider are: the bore of the pipe and the material of which it is made (so that it will not leak), the imposition of a duty to repair and liability for damage caused by leaking, the depth of the pipe, to make sure that crop growing on the servient land is not hampered; reinstatement of the subsoil and topsoil when the pipe has been laid; reinstatement of any land drains affected by the pipe; and removal of the pipe if it ceases to be used. Removal is particularly important in view of current environmental concerns; if the pipe or cable is left to degrade, it may release toxic materials. The landowner might then be liable on the basis that 'polluter pays'. It should be ensured that building and development on the servient land is not prevented by the pipe's existence (*Goodhart v Hyett* (1884) 25 ChD 182), and if the pipeline is likely to prevent development full compensation should be obtained as part of the consideration for the grant. For example, it was held in *St John's College, Oxford v Thames Water Authority* [1980] 1 EGLR 229 that a water main laid with an average working width of excavation of 22 feet sterilised the whole strip of land through which it passed so far as concerned future building over it. It may be possible to cover this point by saying that the parties will try to agree an alternative route if planning permission for development is later obtained and if the development would be frustrated by the presence of the pipe and providing that in default of agreement the value of the loss of development benefit shall be settled by arbitration.

An unremoved pipe or sewer which has ceased to be used may be overlooked on transmission of title. In *William Sindall plc v Cambridgeshire County Council* [1994] 1 WLR 1016 (CA) such a sewer gave rise to a dispute in which issues as to misrepresentation, fundamental mistake and defect in title were raised. The presence of the sewer was held to be a defect in title.

Future easements
    If the original grant gives the dominant owner a right to divert to a route which remains to be chosen he may be held to have a

future easement and if so his grant should be restricted to the perpetuity period to be a valid one (*Dunn v Blackdown Properties Ltd* [1961] Ch 433). It might, however, be saved by the 'wait and see' provisions of the Perpetuities and Accumulations Act 1964, s 3, even if not expressed to be limited to the perpetuity period, provided that the grant took effect after the date when the Act came into force on 16 July 1964. If a grant were made of a future easement by *A* to *B* the period during which one would 'wait and see' whether the grant were saved by taking effect in possession would be governed by the lives of *A* and *B* plus twenty-one years. There is scanty and conflicting authority on what constitutes a future grant and what constitutes an immediate grant. *Sharpe v Durrant* (1911) 55 SJ 423 should be contrasted with *South-Eastern Railway Co Ltd v Associated Portland Cement Manufacturers (1900) Ltd* [1910] 1 Ch 12. In every case, as a precaution, the grant which has a future element should be limited to the perpetuity period. There is further doubt about whether a grant of a right to use pipes and sewers 'now laid or hereafter to be laid' under the servient land and not limited to the perpetuity period is completely valid, completely invalid, or valid as to those laid at the date of the grant and invalid as to those subsequently laid or to be laid. Can the parties be assumed to have intended that if their grant was not completely effective it was to be partly effective? Cross J said in *Dunn's* case, above, at 440, that if there had been existing sewers at the date of the grant that would have conferred an immediate right to make connections to them in the future, under the *Associated Portland Cement* case. This was an obiter dictum of Cross J. If there were no existing sewers at the date of the grant then the grant would be wholly in the future and should certainly be limited to the perpetuity period. By s 1(1) of the 1964 Act, where an instrument made after the coming into force of the Act so provides, the perpetuity period may be of such duration not exceeding 80 years as the instrument specifies in that behalf.

The interpretation put on s 162(1) of the Law of Property Act 1925 by *Dunn's* case must be borne in mind. The subsection says that the rule against perpetuities does not apply and shall be deemed never to have applied to (inter alia) 'any grant, exception, or reservation of any easements ... for the purpose of ... constructing, laying down, altering, repairing, renewing, cleansing, and maintaining sewers, watercourses, cesspools, gutters, drains, water-pipes, gas-pipes, electric wires or cables or other like works' (para *(d)*(iv)). Cross J said in *Dunn's* case (at 441) that if there was a valid right over property not itself void for perpetuity, ancillary rights of constructing to make the main right effective were not to be void merely because they might be exercised outside the perpetuity period. So the section will save only *ancillary* rights, under the current judicial interpretation. A precedent for connecting into drains on a building site in the future (period limited to 20 years) is given in *Precedents for the Conveyancer*, prec 16–23 p 8099, and for mutual rights on two building plots being created out of a larger one, see prec 19–37, p 9642.

Eavesdrop

Another type of pipe easement is the right to drain the rainwater from premises onto the land of another, by a downspout or gutter. It is prudent for the servient owner to stipulate the extent of the grant precisely. He should say where and how the drainage is to take place. He should also state what is to be drained: if the intention is to permit the drainage of *A*'s outhouse roof onto *B*'s land, the grant should say so expressly and not mention *A*'s premises in general, otherwise *A* could later validly add the drainage from the whole of his roof provided the drain would accommodate it. An express grant without limiting words will not be limited to the use contemplated when the grant was made (*British Railways Board v Glass* [1965] Ch 538).

The grant should make provision for the repair of damage caused to *B*'s servient premises by rainwater from the dominant premises, whether by the natural process of drainage or by overflow. *A* in turn will require a right of access onto *B*'s land to inspect, cleanse and repair the pipe or gutter and will be made responsible for any damage caused in the process of exercising his right. The *Encyclopaedia*, 5th ed, vol 12, p 1269 gives precedents.

Licences

Pipes may be laid in or on someone else's land by virtue of a licence. The nature of licences and their assignment is discussed in Chapter 2/2. A precedent may be found in *Precedents for the Conveyancer*, vol 1, 3034.

The grant of a licence can be similar to the grant of an easement and in drafting the licence it will be useful to bear in mind the considerations relevant to a grant of easement. What is the land to be benefited and the land to be burdened? What is the purpose, the extent and the time of beginning and end? What will the pipe be made of and what materials may be passed down the pipe? Who will repair and eventually remove the pipe and reinstate the land? Is the licence determinable and on what grounds? In the absence of stipulation to the contrary, pipes laid in land become the property of the person in whose land they are laid (*Armstrong v Sheppard & Short Ltd* [1959] 2 All ER 651).

It may be useful to incorporate expressly s 196 of the Law of Property Act 1925 (as amended by the Recorded Delivery Service Act 1962, s 1(1)), which deals with the service of notices, although by s 196(5) the section applies to 'notices required to be served by any instrument affecting property' coming into operation after 1 January 1926, unless the contrary appears. Under the section, a notice sent by registered post or recorded delivery service to the person to be served is deemed duly served if not returned through the post office undelivered.

There can be due service even if the addressee does not receive the letter. In *Re 88 Berkeley Road, London, NW9* [1971] 1 All ER 254 one of two joint tenants caused a notice of severance of the joint tenancy to be sent to the other. The notice was received at the premises by the person who had caused it to be sent and the other claimed not to have seen it. There was held to have been due service on the other.

2 Acquisition by implied grant or reservation

Lord Parker of Waddington said in *Pwllbach Colliery Co Ltd v Woodman* [1915] AC 634, at 646–7, that apart from ways of necessity and continuous and apparent easements (both dealt with later in this section) there are two heads of easements granted by implication.

The first is where the implication arises because the right in question is necessary for the enjoyment of some other right expressly granted. He gave the example that a right to draw water from a spring necessarily includes the right to go on someone's land to the spring for this purpose. He added that the second case depends not on the terms of the grant but on the circumstances under which it is made: the law will imply the grant or reservation of such easements as may be necessary to give effect to the common intention of the parties with reference to the manner or purposes in and for which the land granted or some land retained by the grantor is to be used.

Implied ancillary rights

The grant of an easement is prima facie also the grant of such ancillary rights as are reasonably necessary to its exercise or enjoyment (*Jones v Pritchard* [1908] 1 Ch 630, per Parker J, at 638). The same proposition applies to a right gained not by grant but by prescription. In *Roberts v Fellowes* (1906) 94 LT 279, a person who had a prescriptive right to a flow of water to his mill over the defendant's land, along a stream the banks of which had been artificially built up to maintain the flow, was held entitled to enter onto the defendant's land to repair the banks when they were undermined by rats and moles. A grant of a right to lay pipes in another's land carries with it the right to enter on the land to repair the pipes: *Pomfret v Ricroft* (1669) 1 Wms Saund 321 (6th ed), at 323 (explicable also, however, on the principle of non-derogation from grant). Indeed, there is a duty on the owner of the pipe easement to keep his pipes in repair: *Humphries v Cousins* (1877) 2 CPD 239 (occupier of house held liable when his drain, which ran under a neighbour's public-house, leaked and caused damage there). A right to pass and repass on foot along a way does not carry an ancillary right to lay flexible pipes along the way to empty a cess-pit of sewage (*Penn v Wilkins* (1974) 236 EG 203).

Many modern property developments include projecting upper level pedestrian footways. If the developer does not own the land over which the pedestrian way extends, he will need a grant of an easement to project into the air-space which it occupies. It is suggested that he will by implication (if it is not granted expressly) acquire ancillary easements to lead drainage pipes down to ground level and to enter onto the ground floor land when required to repair the elevated way and its supports and pipes.

Has a pipe laid in land a right of support and protection from the soil in which it is laid? In *Newcastle-under-Lyme Corporation v Wolstanton Ltd* [1947] Ch 427 (a case where pipes were laid under statutory authority) it was held that the pipe-owners gained no right of ownership in respect of the soil in which the pipes were laid but they had a right to occupy that cavity which their pipes filled; their only right to support was an implied one (which in this case had been taken away by statute). Where the pipes are laid by private grant or under prescription it is suggested that the dominant owner will be entitled to have his pipes supported by the land over which they run (and protected by the soil if the nature of the pipe and its contents require it), or if not by the land then by an adequate substitute. Support and protection are ancillary rights necessary to the enjoyment of the pipe easement (*Jones v Pritchard* [1908] 1 Ch 630, at 638). A person has no right apart from agreement to have his pipes supported by the water which is under the land in which the pipes run (*Popplewell v Hodkinson* [1861–73] All ER Rep 999), but he can object if the support afforded by wet sand (*Jordeson v Sutton, Southcoats and Drypool Gas Co* (1899) 2 Ch 217) or brine (*Lotus v British Soda Co Ltd* [1972] Ch 123) is removed.

The rights to repair pipes and to replace with other pipes when deterioration makes it necessary are obviously ancillary to the grant to the dominant owner. The right to substitute an improved type of pipe or cable will be included in the right to lay. All these will require access and, provided the disturbance caused to the servient owner is not unreasonable and is made good, he will not be entitled to complain. Indeed, if the dominant owner does not keep his pipe in repair, so that water escapes onto the servient land, he will be liable in trespass to the servient owner (*Jones v Pritchard*, above, at 638; *Humphries v Cousins*, above).

By contrast, apart from any special local custom or express contract, the owner of a servient tenement is not under any obligation to the owner of the dominant tenement to execute any repairs necessary to ensure the enjoyment of the easement by the dominant owner (*Duke of Westminster v Gould* (1983) 267 EG 762 (CA)). But where the defect on the servient tenement amounts to a nuisance the servient owner is liable to the dominant owner if he does not take reasonable steps to abate it: *Leakey v National Trust* [1980] QB 485 (CA) (landslip); *Bradburn v Lindsay* [1983] 2 All ER 408 (dry rot and disrepair).

The owner of land over which there is a right of way owes no duty of care, at common law or under the Occupier's Liability Act 1957; persons lawfully using the way are not necessarily the occupier's 'visitors' (*Holden v White* [1982] 2 WLR 1030 (CA)).

It is a question of degree in every case whether the right claimed is reasonably ancillary to the right granted. For example, if a person is granted the right to construct a tunnel through his neighbour's embankment to reach the main road from his own land and he uses the tunnel as a garage for his vehicles, he could be restrained. Parking for a brief period whilst he shuts the gate from the main road, for example, would be ancillary to the grant;

garaging would not (*Bulstrode v Lambert* [1953] 1 WLR 1064, at 1071).

Where there is a right to have a pipe running through another's land there is an ancillary right with it to prevent him from doing anything on his land which will make the exercise of the ancillary right of repair substantially more difficult than formerly (*Goodhart v Hyett* (1884) 25 ChD 182).

Common intention of parties: implied grant or reservation

Wilde B said in *Hall v Lund* (1863) 1 H & C 676, at 685–6, that in cases of implied grant the implication must be confined to a reasonable use of the premises for the purpose for which, according to the obvious intention of the parties, they are demised; each case must depend on its own circumstances and the intention of the parties to be ascertained from the character, state and use of the premises at the time of the grant. For example, in *Ewart v Cochrane* (1861) 5 LT 1, a house adjoined a tan yard and both were owned by the same person. The tan yard was drained by a gutter into a cesspool in one corner of the garden of the house. Then the tan yard was sold off and the system of drainage continued. When the house was sold its purchaser sought to prevent the drainage. It was held that the right to use the drain became an easement on severance and passed by implied grant as it was necessary for the convenient and comfortable enjoyment of the tan yard. (This does not mean that there was an 'easement of necessity'. 'Necessity' has a narrower meaning than 'necessary': *Union Lighterage Co v London Graving Dock Co* [1902] 2 ChD 557, per Stirling LJ, at 573.)

An implied easement may arise where properties are severed by being devised by will to separate persons. In *Schwann v Cotton* [1916] 2 Ch 459, three adjoining properties, *A*, *B* and *C* were served with water by a pipe running underground from a well on *A*. The testator, who owned *B* and *C*, devised them to different persons, who in turn sold to Cotton and Schwann respectively. Cotton stopped up the flow of the pipe to *C* and Schwann claimed successfully an implied right to have the flow continued.

The rule in Wheeldon v Burrows

Where the ownership of adjoining premises is severed the rule in *Wheeldon v Burrows* (1879) 12 ChD 31 is frequently important. It was in this case laid down that on a severance of ownership the grantee will obtain by implication all those continuous and apparent easements which are necessary to his reasonable enjoyment of the property granted *and* which were enjoyed by the grantor (as quasi-easements) before severance. *Ewart v Cochrane*, above, though decided before *Wheeldon v Burrows*, is an example of the application of the principle. In *Watts v Kelson* (1871) 6 Ch App 166, a person who had two pieces of land made a water supply to the second from a tank on the first. He sold off the second, and then the first. It was held that the owner of the second could insist on the continuance of the supply from the first. It will be a question of fact in each case what easements are reasonably necessary, whether they have been 'continuous and apparent' (ie, evidence of their existence can be seen on inspection) and whether they were enjoyed by the vendor at the time of severance. The fact that a pipe was temporarily blocked at the time of severance or had burst in a recent frost would not prevent the right to use it from passing by implication. The case would be otherwise if it had been blocked or burst many years earlier and had not been used since. No right will pass by implication under the rule in *Wheeldon v Burrows* if the grantor was incapable of making an express grant of the easement in question; see *Re St Clements, Leigh-on-Sea* [1988] 1 WLR 720 (incumbent of church unable to grant claimed right of way without a faculty from the ecclesiastical court).

For the effect of the Standard Conditions of Sale of Land (2nd ed 1992) on the grant or reservation of easements on a sale-off of land, see below.

Implied reservation

Wheeldon v Burrows, above, will not imply reservations in favour of a grantor; if the vendor wishes to reserve any rights out of the property to be conveyed he must do so expressly (Thesiger LJ, at 49; *Cordell v Second Clanfield Properties Ltd* [1969] 2 Ch 9). So if *A* grants a right to *B* to lay and use a drain under *A*'s land, *A* cannot then grant to *C* a right to tie into and use the drain laid by *B*, unless *A* reserved against *B* the right to make such a grant (*Simmons v Midford* [1969] 2 Ch 415). The only case in which an easement may be reserved in favour of a grantor is where he can claim an easement of necessity. To do this he will have to establish that without the easement the property retained cannot be used at all, not merely that inconvenience would be caused to him if he did not have it (*Union Lighterage Co v London Graving Dock Co* [1902] 2 Ch 557, at 573, per Stirling LJ). An obvious example is where the owner sells some land and leaves himself with an insufficient way to carry on his existing business (*Gayford v Moffatt* (1868) 4 Ch App 133). But rights to a supply of water and to drain away foul water over the property sold are equally important and it appears that they would be held to be easements of necessity. In *Williams v Usherwood* (1983) 45 P & CR 235 (CA) it was held that where an adverse possessor established a possessory title to the surface of land he could be subject to the rights of the paper owner, which had the practical characteristics of easements, as necessities. Thus the adverse possessor gained title to the former dominant land but remained subject to the former owner's right to go onto it for maintaining his property and the right to continue to use the drains under it, which led into the drains common to both properties. In *Wong v Beaumont Property Trust Ltd* [1965] 1 QB 173 (CA), a claim to fix a ventilation duct on the servient land, without which duct the public health authorities would close the kitchens of the dominant premises (a restaurant), was held to be a valid claim to an easement of necessity. So if the 'drainage' of smells and fumes could be upheld, so could any other essential drainage claim. It was held in *Holmes v Goring* (1824) 2 Bing 76, that a way of necessity does not survive the necessity which gives rise to it and will cease if the person who has a way of necessity to his property acquires another access to it. The decision was doubted in *Proctor v Hodgson* (1855) 10 Exch 824.

The Court of Appeal in *Nickerson v Barraclough* [1981] 2 WLR 773 disagreed with the view that easements of necessity are based upon public policy. They are based upon implication from the circumstances at the time of the grant. Public policy has no part to play in construing the instrument, though it may require the court to frustrate the parties' intentions when they have been ascertained. If it is clear that without the implication of an easement land is unusable or of little use, that may be an indication that the parties intended it to have an easement, such as one of drainage or ventilation, over the grantor's adjoining land. A declaration excluding or limiting the grant of an easement will not be overruled on the ground that the land could be more fully or more profitably used if the exclusion were removed. An easement of necessity will only be implied into a conveyance of land where without such an easement the property retained could not be used at all. It will not be allowed simply where it is necessary to the reasonable enjoyment of the property, *MRA Engineering Ltd v Trimster Co Ltd* (1988) 56 P & CR 1 (CA).

Where the easements claimed are complex and would require to be discussed and negotiated they are unlikely to be allowed by the court under the doctrine of necessity (*Sovmots Investments Ltd v Secretary of State* [1979] AC 144 (HL); claim for series of easements for maisonettes in a large tower block development).

Where there are drains used in common by adjoining houses and running under both and the ownership is severed, each house will acquire the right to use the drains running under the other, but will be subject to the similar rights of the other (*Pyer v Carter* (1857) 1 H & N 916). This situation only arises where the drainage from *A* runs onto *B*, joins with the drainage from *B* and then comes back under *A*.

When the owner of two properties sells them at the same time to different purchasers who know of the contemporaneous sales, then each acquires the continuous and apparent easements over the other's land which existed as quasi-easements before severance (*Allen v Taylor* (1880–81) 16 ChD 355). Rights to drainage and to a supply of water are examples of such mutual rights.

Law of Property Act, s 62

Section 62(1) of the Law of Property Act 1925 says that a conveyance of land shall be deemed to include and shall convey (inter alia) all ditches, waters, watercourses, liberties, privileges, easements, rights and advantages whatsoever appertaining or reputed to appertain to the land at the time of the conveyance. By s 62(2) a conveyance of land, having houses or other buildings thereon, shall be deemed to include and shall convey with the land (inter alia) all cisterns, sewers, gutters, drains, watercourses, liberties, privileges, rights and advantages whatsoever appertaining or reputed to appertain to the land or buildings at the time of the conveyance. By subs (4) the section will only apply to the extent that a contrary intention is not expressed in the conveyance, and by subs (6) the section applies only to conveyances made after 31 December 1881. 'Conveyance' is widely defined in s 205(1)(ii). The effect of s 62 is that on a conveyance rights corresponding to the benefits enjoyed before the conveyance can come into existence although they would not be deemed to arise under the rule in *Wheeldon v Burrows*, above, because that rule requires the enjoyment of the quasi-easement before severance to have been continuous and apparent or necessary to the reasonable enjoyment of the land granted. It is a requirement under s 62 that the right claimed should have been enjoyed with the land conveyed at the time of the conveyance. It was held in *Handel v St Stephens Close Ltd* [1994] 1 EGLR 70 that where tenants of a block of flats had parked their cars on the private roads of the grounds of the flats for many years, an injunction against withdrawing the facility would be granted. Issues of estoppel and the application of the Law of Property Act 1925, s 62(2), arose.

The permitted use of drainage facilities could raise similar issues. Section 62 and the rule in *Wheeldon v Burrows* can only apply where the conveying party owns the quasi-servient tenement at the time he conveys away the quasi-dominant tenement, *MRA Engineering Ltd v Trimster Co Ltd* (1988) 56 P & CR 1 (CA). An example of the wide operation of s 62 is provided by *Goldberg v Edwards* [1950] Ch 247, where a person who had agreed to take a lease and had gone into possession was allowed to use a passage to a particular exit as an alternative to the usual passage. When the lease had formally been granted he successfully claimed that under s 62 he had a legal right of way along the passage. The section will not operate to grant rights in property unknown to the law, such as a right to take water from an artificial watercourse whenever the owner of it chooses to let water flow along it (*Burrows v Lang* [1902] 2 Ch 502), or a claim to personal services (*Regis Property Co Ltd v Redman* [1956] 2 QB 612), nor will it convert into a right a permission intended when granted to be only temporary (*Wright v Macadam* [1949] 2 KB 744 (CA); *Green v Ashco Horticulturist Ltd* [1966] 1 WLR 889).

Once a right has passed to another under s 62(1), it will be a legal easement and bind a successor in title irrespective of notice, as illustrated in *Robins v Tupman* [1993] 1 EGLR 169 (CA) (sale-off of part of property included right to drain into soakaway on land retained; when retained land was sold, purchaser was bound by easement).

In *Sovmots Investments Ltd v Secretary of State* [1979] AC 144 (HL) it was held that no easements could be implied under s 62 in respect of maisonettes forming part of a tower development when the maisonettes had not been occupied before the local authority acquired them, as no rights appertained to them before severance. The effect of this decision was limited by the Local Government (Miscellaneous Provisions) Act 1976, s 13 and Sched 1, which provided from 14 February 1977 that on a compulsory acquisition of land a local authority might acquire 'new rights' not in existence when the order specifying them is made. The authority declared what the rights were to be and at the same time acquired them. Several other statutes now contain similar convenient provisions, for example, the Water Industry Act 1991, s 155(2) and Sched 9.

In *Nickerson v Barraclough* [1981] 2 WLR 773 (CA) it was held that where a way passed under s 62(1) for agricultural and sporting purposes it could not later be used for building purposes when the owner of the easement acquired further land adjacent to the original dominant tenement.

Necessary ancillary rights will be implied. In the case of *Morris v Cartwright* (1963) 107 SJ 553, a person to whom a right to a supply of water from adjoining land had passed under s 62 was held entitled to the ancillary right to go onto the servient land to repair the system of pipes to continue his supply.

Where land is sold off under the terms of the Standard Conditions of Sale of Land (2nd ed, 1992) and the seller retains land near the property, a Condition says:

> 3.3.2 The buyer will have no right of light or air over the retained land, but otherwise the seller and the buyer will each have the rights over the land of the other which they would have had if they were two separate buyers to whom the seller had made simultaneous transfers of the property and retained land.
> 3.3.3 Either party may require that the transfer contain appropriate express terms.

This imports the rule applicable to simultaneous sales-off under *Swansborough v Coventry* (1832) 2 Moo & S 362 and gives the seller benefits which he would not obtain otherwise at common law, because the view was taken in *Wheeldon v Burrows* (1879) 12 ChD 31 that the seller acquires no rights by implication on a sale-off and must expressly reserve those he wishes to have.

Easements supplied by statute

Where a tenant purchases the freehold under the provisions of the Leasehold Reform Act 1967, the conveyance to him has by implication the effect of granting with the premises (inter alia) rights of passage of water, gas or other piped fuel over adjoining land, and of drainage, so as to secure to the premises the same benefits as were enjoyed under the tenancy (s 10(2)(i)). The premises are subject to similar burdens for the benefit of adjoining premises (s 10(2)(ii)). The conveyance must not exclude the operation of the Law of Property Act 1925, s 62 unless the tenant/ purchaser consents (s 10(1)).

Similar provisions apply on a conveyance to a nominee purchaser on enfranchisement under the Leasehold Reform, Housing and Urban Development Act 1993, s 34 and Sched 7.

Where a secure tenant of a house purchases it under the 'right-to-buy' provisions of the Housing Act 1985, Sched 6 sets out the provisions which are to be incorporated in the conveyance of the freehold, or the grant of the lease, as the case may be (s 139). In certain cases the Housing Act 1988 s 79 and Sched 11 (disposal of land by a housing action trust) may also be relevant.

By the 1985 Act, Pt I of Sched 6, para 1, the conveyance or grant 'shall not exclude or restrict the general words implied under s 62 of the Law of Property Act 1925 unless the tenant consents or the exclusion or restriction is made for the purpose of preserving or recognising any existing interest of the landlord in tenant's incumbrances or any existing right or interest of any other person'.

By para 2 the conveyance or grant shall have the effect of granting with the house all the rights which the tenant previously enjoyed from adjoining property but make him subject to all such easements and rights for the benefit of other property as are capable of existing in law and are necessary to secure to the persons interested in the other property the same rights as were available before the sale. These rights are rights of support; access of light and air; passage of water, gas or other piped fuel; the drainage or disposal of water, sewage, smoke or fumes; the use of or maintenance of pipes or other installations for such passage, drainage or disposal; and rights to the use or maintenance of cables for the supply of electricity, telephone 'or the receipt directly or by landline of visual or other wireless signals' (para 2(1)). Where a lease is granted there are to be covenants by the parties, including one of the landlord to keep in repair structure and exterior (including drains, gutters and external pipes) and another to maintain services at a reasonable level and to keep in repair the installations for the provision of those services (para 14). Where the property sold is a flat, there are covenants implied by the landlord to keep the structure and exterior (including drains, gutters and external pipes) in repair, para 14.

A standard conveyance for a sale under the 1980 Act (now the 1985 Act) is given in *Precedents for the Conveyancer*, vol 2, 8141.

Under the London Building Acts 1930 to 1982 adjoining owners have the right (for example) to underpin, demolish or repair party walls and to enter onto neighbouring land to do so and necessary dealings with pipes and cables would no doubt be ancillary to this right. However the due procedures as to the giving of notice must be given, otherwise the work can be restrained by injunction, *London and Manchester Assurance Co Ltd v O & H Construction Ltd* (1988) EGCS 41, applying *Anchor Brewhouse Developments Ltd v Berkley House (Docklands Developments) Ltd* [1987] 2 EGLR 173. Bristol has similar local legislation.

The Access to Neighbouring Land Act 1992 provides in default of agreement for a person to obtain a court 'access order' allowing access to neighbouring land for the purpose of carrying out preservation works to his own land (such as for repairing a wall). The order will state the works to be done, the area to be entered and the period of the permission. Compensation for damage caused to the neighbouring land or for 'substantial loss of privacy or other substantial inconvenience' is payable. The works must be 'reasonably necessary for the preservation of the whole or any part of the dominant land'. Thus a proposal to lay a new pipe, drain, cable or sewer through a neighbour's land (as distinct from a replacement) will require agreement and cannot be ordered under the Act unless it falls within the phrase 'basic preservation works' defined in s 1(4)(*b*). The Act took effect on 31 January 1993.

Extent of the implied rights

The extent of the grant will be ascertained from the implication of a reasonable use for the purpose, according to the obvious intention of the parties, for which the premises are conveyed; the character, state and use of the premises at the time of the grant will be a help in ascertaining intention (*Hall v Lund* (1863) 1 H & C 676). In this case a lease of a mill was made to Lund. The lessor owned two mills. The one leased was drained through an artificial drain into a natural watercourse which supplied the other mill. The lessee's predecessor, Pullan, had been a bleacher and had drained the waste products from his process into the watercourse. The lease described the premises as 'late in the occupation of Pullan'. Lund was also a bleacher and continued the drainage. The lessor sold the other mill, and the purchaser, who carried on the business of a paper manufacturer, sought to forbid Lund's practice. He was unsuccessful, as it was held that there was an implied grant to Lund to continue to drain his bleaching business as Pullan had done, to the extent that Pullan and he had done before the purchaser bought the lessor's mill.

In *Watts v Kelson* (1871) 6 Ch App 166, a person was held to be entitled to a supply of pipe-water to his land from other land formerly in the same ownership. The supply had originally been to cattle sheds on the land. The claim was upheld for a supply of water to a house which was built in place of the sheds; granted the existence of the right, the use to which the water was put was irrelevant in this case. But it is suggested that, if a large block of flats had been erected in place of the cattle sheds and the owner of them had claimed a right to the greatly increased quantity of water which they required, he would have been unsuccessful because the intention to supply such an amount of water could not have been in the minds of the parties at the date of the original grant of the land. The volume required must at some stage so far exceed that originally supplied that a matter of degree turns into a difference in principle. This would certainly be so if the volume demanded would require the installation of a much larger water-pipe.

The position would be otherwise if the grant were an express, and not an implied one. An express grant which contains no limiting words will not be restricted to the grant contemplated when the grant is made (*British Railways Board v Glass* [1965] Ch 538). The flats in the example would be entitled to as much water as the original pipe could supply; a wide grant might even extend to permit a supply through a substituted larger pipe, as it was held in *Bulstrode v Lambert* [1953] 1 WLR 1064 (a case on a right of way) that the wide wording of a grant permitted the dominant owner to remove posts which narrowed the way and to use it thereafter for larger vehicles than had ever used it before. From that adaptation of the way it is not a big step to the enlargement of a pipe. See also *Keefe v Amor* [1965] 1 QB 334 (CA).

The easements impliedly granted under an enfranchisement under the Leasehold Reform Act 1967 are such as 'are necessary to secure to the tenant as nearly as may be the same rights as . . . were available to him under . . . the tenancy' (s 10(2)(i)). Rights are also impliedly reserved to the landlord on the same basis (s 10(2)(ii)). Similar provisions operate on a conveyance to a nominee purchaser on enfranchisement under the Leasehold Reform, Housing and Urban Development Act 1993, s 34 and Sched 7.

3 Acquisition by prescription

A person who enjoys a benefit which has the necessary characteristics of an easement over the land of another can establish a right by prescription to the easement if he can show a right either at common law under a presumed grant or under the doctrine of lost modern grant or under the Prescription Act 1832.

Presumed grant

The right at common law depends on the claimant being able to show that he claims under a grant made before 1189. If he can show enjoyment throughout the memory of living persons he will raise a presumption of an ancient grant, as he will also be showing twenty years' user (*Bealey v Shaw* (1805) 6 East 208, per Lord Ellenborough CJ, at 215). But his claim can be defeated by proof that the right could not have existed in 1189, for example, by showing that a house which claims a right of drainage through the servient land was built on land which was farmland in, say, 1850. The title deeds are obviously vital here. The claim will also be defeated by evidence of enjoyment by licence, perhaps by payment of an acknowledgement rent by the claimant (*Gardner v Hodgson's Kingston Brewery Co Ltd* [1903] AC 229); by showing that since 1189 the dominant and servient lands were in the same ownership, thus extinguishing the right by unity of seisin (*Damper v Bassett* [1901] 2 Ch 350); by showing enjoyment by force, secrecy or fraud (*Sturges v Bridgman* (1879) 11 ChD 852, at 863); or by showing that the enjoyment was not continuous (*Hollins v Verney* (1883–84) 13 QBD 304: the use of a way for hauling timber in 1851–53, again in 1866–68, and again in 1881 held to be insufficient assertion of a continuous right to enjoyment).

Lost modern grant

'The basis on which the court is entitled to make the presumption of the lost modern grant . . . is that the owner of the allegedly servient tenement or a predecessor in title has, with knowledge of acts which would otherwise be acts of trespass, acquiesced in those acts and, therefore, it must be assumed that the owner of the servient tenement or some predecessor in title of his has given his consent in the proper way, namely by a deed of grant of that easement' (Megaw LJ in *Oakley v Boston* [1975] QB 271 (CA) at

280). The proof will vary with the right claimed and evidence of user of upwards of twenty years is usually sufficient (*Tehidy Minerals Ltd v Norman* [1971] 2 QB 182 (CA)). A claim will fail if it can be shown that there was never a competent grantor (*Neaverson v Peterborough Rural District Council* [1902] 1 Ch 557) or grantee. In *Oakley v Boston*, above, it was held that an incumbent of a parish had power under the Ecclesiastical Leasing Acts 1842 and 1858 to grant an easement over glebe land but that the consent of the Ecclesiastical Commissioners was needed and the consent could not be presumed in the absence of any evidence of its being granted.

A grant cannot be presumed for an illegal purpose, such as to pollute a river contrary to statute (*Hulley v Silversprings Bleaching & Dyeing Co Ltd* [1922] 2 Ch 268). As in the case of a common law claim, force, secrecy, fraud, licence, unity of ownership and interruption can defeat the claim. Involuntary interruption, such as by requisitioning and use under licence from the requisitioning authority, will not affect the claim (*Tehidy Minerals Ltd v Norman*, above). Since the user is under lost grant the enjoyment does not have to be 'next before action brought' as in the claim under prescription (see s 4 of the Prescription Act 1832): in *Oakley v Boston*, above, a successful claim was made even though user had been continuous from 1927 to 1962 and intermittent from 1962 to the commencement of the action in 1973. An easement may be acquired under the doctrine of lost modern grant even if the dominant and servient owners have the mistaken belief that the enjoyment of the 'easement' is by express grant made when the respective properties were erected; *Bridle v Ruby* [1988] 3 WLR 191 (CA) (use of driveway of adjoining house for access to garage, right to use the drive in original conveyance but clause deleted).

Prescription Act 1832

The Prescription Act 1832 does not alter the common law but it sets out standards by which the effect of the enjoyment of alleged rights can be judged. Section 2 states that no claim at common law by custom, prescription or grant to 'any way or other easement, or to any watercourse, or to the use of any water' if enjoyed without interruption for twenty years before the action was brought, shall be defeated by showing only that it was first enjoyed at a time prior to 20 years before the action. The effect of this is that if a person shows 20 years' continuous enjoyment of an alleged right, evidence that no such right was enjoyed 21 years ago will not defeat his claim to an easement. The claim could be defeated by other defences, however, such as secret or violent enjoyment or permission. The section goes on to say that where there is shown 40 years' enjoyment without interruption before the action the right shall be deemed 'absolute and indefeasible, unless it shall appear that the same was enjoyed by some consent or agreement expressly given or made for that purpose by deed or writing'. Again, the user must be as of right to be valid. The section does not apply to claims to a right of light, which must be established under s 3. The peculiar phrase in s 2 'to any way or other easement, or to any watercourse, or the use of any water' seems to imply that a claim to a watercourse or use of water is not an easement, and the phrase 'way or other easement' could be read under the ejusdem generis rule as 'way or other easement in the nature of a way'. It has been said, however, that the section applies to all easements (*Dalton v Angus* (1880–1) 6 App Cas 740, per Lord Selbourne LC, at 798). A right to divert a watercourse (*Mason v Shrewsbury and Hereford Railway Co* (1871) LR 6 QB 578) and a right to pollute a watercourse (*Wright v Williams* (1836) 1 M & W 77) have been recognised under the section.

If the claimant shows user for a less period than the twenty or forty years, no presumption can be made from this alone in support of a claim (s 6) but the court might still find from all the circumstances evidence of an implied grant (*Hanmer v Chance* (1865) 4 De GJ & Sm 626). It is an open question whether, if a period of user commences upon an express but verbal agreement inconsistent with prescription, the person enjoying it can after twenty years' enjoyment claim an easement by prescription. In *Reilly v Orange* [1955] 2 QB 112 a right of way to premises was granted verbally to last until the grantee should have made an access over his own land to the premises. He claimed an easement by prescription. He failed on insufficient length of enjoyment, so the question put did not arise, but Jenkins LJ, at 118–19, doubted whether an easement could arise contrary to the plain intention of the parties when the permission was given. It is suggested that, as enjoyment under a claim by prescription must be enjoyment 'as of right,' no easement could arise by user under an intended temporary and conditional permission such as was given in this case. Support for this view is provided by *Hughes v Griffin* [1969] 1 WLR 23 (CA): there the owner of a house conveyed it as a gift to his nephew in 1951, but remained living there until his death in 1965. His widow claimed that he had re-acquired the title to the property from the nephew by adverse possession: it was held that his possession from 1951 was by licence and so was not 'adverse' and time never began to run. But it is possible for a user which began as permissive to change its character and become adverse, so that time starts to run (*Healey v Hawkins* [1968] 1 WLR 1967).

In computing the 20 or 40 year period, any period of interruption which lasts for less than one year is to be disregarded (s 4). The full period of enjoyment must be shown to have passed (*Reilly v Orange*, above) and to continue up to the date when the action calling the alleged right into question is commenced (s 4). The commencement of an action concerning the right is not an 'interruption' within s 4 (*Reilly v Orange*). In *Newnham v Willson* (1988) 56 P & CR 8 (CA) a person had used a driveway from 1960 until it was deliberately obstructed by the defendants in spring 1983 and on 23 June 1983 the plaintiff's solicitors wrote to protest about the obstruction. The plaintiff commenced proceedings on 27 June 1984 but failed as there had been an interruption lasting more than a year, from March 1983, so there had not been user for 20 years 'next before some suit or action' under the Prescription Act 1832, s 4. If the right claimed has been enjoyed for only 19 years and one day, the objector is too late to interrupt it because his interruption cannot last for one year before the 20 year period is up (*Flight v Thomas* (1841) 8 Cl & Fin 231). The claimant of the easement should not make the mistake, however, of starting his action before 20 years' enjoyment has gone by, because he will fail under the plain words of s 2, which require him to show 20 years' enjoyment (*Reilly v Orange*).

The prescription period is not necessarily interrupted if the route of the easement being gained is altered during the period of acquisition: *Davis v Whitby* [1974] Ch 186 (CA) (one way used for 15 years: another way nearby substituted for it and used for 18 years: valid easement acquired).

Any period during which the person capable of objecting to the user is under disability, being 'an infant, idiot, *non compos mentis, feme covert*, or tenant for life', is excluded from the computation of the prescription period where the claim is for the easement by reason of 20 years' enjoyment, but not where it is a claim by reason of 40 years' enjoyment (s 7).

Where there is 'any land or water upon, over or from which any way or other convenient (a possible misprint for 'easement': *Wright v Williams* (1836) 1 M & W 77) watercourse or use of water shall have been or shall be enjoyed or derived', s 8 applies. Under the section, where the alleged servient tenement has been held by a life tenant or for a lease exceeding three years, then the period of the life interest or tenancy is disregarded in computing 40 year enjoyment provided that the person entitled to the reversion commences his action claiming that there is no prescriptive easement within three years of the cessation of the life interest or lease. The section does not apply to a claim based on 20 years' enjoyment, so if there is such a claim the fact that the servient land is leased for part of the time is irrelevant: *Palk v Shinner* (1852) 18 QB 568 (a good claim to an easement by 20 years' enjoyment even though the land had been tenanted for all but the last five years of the 20).

No easement can be acquired by prescription against a servient owner who has no power to make express grants, such as a company for which a grant would be ultra vires (*Rochdale Canal Co v Radcliffe* (1852) 18 QB 287). Similarly, an alleged dominant owner with no power to acquire an interest in land (*National Guaranteed Manure Co Ltd v Donald* (1859) 4 H & N 8), or a vague body of people, cannot prescribe. A tenant can prescribe for the benefit of his landlord as his enjoyment is that of his landlord (*Gayford v Moffatt* (1868) 4 Ch App 133; *Pugh v Savage* [1970] 2 QB 373 (CA)), but not for his own benefit.

An easement cannot be acquired by conduct which, at the time that the conduct took place, was prohibited by public statute (*Hanning v Top Deck Travel Group Ltd* (1994) 68 P & CR 14 (CA); claim to an easement of way over manorial waste land, forbidden by s 193 of the Law of Property Act 1925).

Nature and extent of prescription

The user required to establish an easement must be such as to indicate throughout the statutory period to a reasonable person in occupation of the servient land that a continuous right to enjoyment is being asserted (*Hollins v Verney* (1883–4) 13 QBD 304, at 315). So a benefit enjoyed secretly, or by force, or fraudulently over the servient land for the necessary period will not establish a claim to an easement. In *Liverpool Corporation v Coghill & Son Ltd* [1918] 1 Ch 307, the claimants discharged borax solution intermittently and usually at night into the Corporation's sewers, unknown to the Corporation, for over 20 years. Their claim to have an easement to do so failed. Enjoyment by permission will be fatal to a claim (*Healey v Hawkins* [1968] 1 WLR 1967) unless the permission was limited and had ended. In *Wood v Waud* (1849) 3 Ex 748, a person claimed an easement to have water flow through his land along an underground artificial channel. The water was pumped off to drain a nearby colliery owned by his neighbour. It was held that he had no right to insist on the colliery owner draining his mine through the channel, so his enjoyment was permissive and precarious only. Prescription depends on the presumption or inference of a grant because of the knowledge and acquiescence of the servient owner (*Dalton v Angus* (1880–1) 6 App Cas 740, per Fry J, at 773). The knowledge of the servient owner concerning the user may be actual (he observes what is done, he has the means to prevent it and he does not do so) or constructive (he may be presumed to have known of the user, or he has had a reasonable opportunity of knowing, and he was able to prevent it and did not do so): *Lloyds Bank Ltd v Dalton* [1942] Ch 466. In *Diment v N H Foot Ltd* [1974] 1 WLR 1427 it was held that the fact that a surveyor arranged tenancies and collected rents of a farm was insufficient to fix the owner with knowledge that a way was being used across the farm by an adjoining landowner.

A prescriptive right in excess of his natural rights may be obtained in respect of water flowing in a natural stream by a riparian owner. The natural right is to use the stream water for ordinary purposes connected with the riparian property, such as watering his cattle, and for extraordinary purposes provided these are connected with the landowner's enjoyment of his riparian land and the water is restored to the stream substantially undiminished in volume and unaltered in character (*McCartney v Londonderry and Lough Swilly Railway Co Ltd* [1904] AC 301). The use of river water by a riparian owner for spray-irrigation of his crops, a method which took 60,000 gallons a day and resulted in not more than 4 per cent of the water returning into the river eventually, was held to be a non-permissible purpose as against a lower riparian owner in *Rugby Joint Water Board v Walters* [1967] Ch 397. Examples of prescriptive rights are a right against a lower riparian owner to pollute the water (*McIntyre Brothers v McGavin* [1893] AC 268) and a right to divert water from a lower owner (*Mason v Shrewsbury and Hereford Railway Co* (1870–71) LR 6 QB 578).

In *Scott-Whitehead v National Coal Board* (1987) 53 P & CR 263 it was held that:

(a) a riparian owner has a natural right to have water in any channel which flows through or abuts upon his land in its natural state both as regards purity and quantity;

(b) as against a party who is *not* also a riparian owner, this right is not affected by the use made of the water by the riparian owner, even if he uses it for irrigation and not for domestic purposes and even if he does not substantially return the water to the river after use;

(c) a riparian owner can acquire a right by prescription to take water of a certain quality from a stream (for example, water of which the chlorine content does not exceed safe levels) and any appreciable worsening of its state will infringe his prescriptive right;

(d) a defendant who wishes to rely upon the right by prescription to pollute a stream must show that his pollution at the time complained of does not exceed that committed during the period of his acquisition of the alleged prescriptive right;

(e) a water authority which knowingly admits into the stream quantities of salt which it must know could be harmful to riparian owners' crops owes a duty of care to the riparian owners to warn them and/or to act with reasonable dispatch to divert the water from them.

Even though a person has acquired a prescriptive right to abstract or impound water he still needs a licence, under the Water Resources Act 1991, from the National Rivers Authority before he may abstract water from a source of supply (s 24(1)). By s 27 of the Water Resources Act 1991, an occupier of land which is contiguous to the water at the place where the abstraction is effected may abstract without a licence for domestic or agricultural purposes (but not for spray-irrigation without a licence). A licence is not needed for an abstraction not exceeding 20 cubic metres, if it does not form part of a continuous operation, or a series of operations, whereby in the aggregate more than 20 cubic metres is abstracted (s 27(2)). In *Cargill v Gotts* [1981] 1 WLR 441 it was held that s 24(1) of the Water Resources Act 1963, the predecessor to s 27, did not authorise a person to abstract as much water as he pleased from any one source of supply, provided only that each abstraction did not exceed 20 cubic metres. Large abstractions taken piecemeal might amount to a series of operations and fall within s 22(2). If a person has a licence to abstract under the Water Resources Act 1991 or a predecessor Act and complies with it, he has a defence to any action brought either by the river authority or a lower riparian owner in respect of his abstraction of water, per Stuart-Smith J in *Scott-Whitehead v NCB* (above).

An easement of eavesdrop for water from a house roof to be discharged onto adjoining land can be acquired by prescription (*Thomas v Thomas* (1835) 2 Cr M & R 34).

Prescriptive rights can be acquired in respect of artificial watercourses provided that the court is satisfied that the watercourse is a permanent one. If it is constructed for a temporary purpose, such as to be enjoyed during the continuance of a lease, no easement can be prescribed for because no easement could have been intended or expressly granted by the parties (*Chamber Colliery Co v Hopwood* (1886) 32 ChD 549). Length of enjoyment is not conclusive; a flow of water from 1771 to 1836 over a man's land was held not to give him a prescriptive right to have it continued (*Arkwright v Gell* (1839) 5 M & W 203). A 'temporary purpose' is one which in the reasonable contemplation of the parties may come to an end; it is a user which is not meant to be a permanent alteration of the face of nature (*Burrows v Lang* [1901] 2 Ch 502, per Farwell J, at 508). The purpose served by the artificial watercourse will often indicate whether it is a temporary one. A polythene pipe laid to supply water to a construction site is apparently temporary, to be used only until the building work is done, and so are drains from prefabricated office buildings on the site. A substantial pipe laid carefully and connected to the plumbing system of the building erected on the site is apparently a permanent artificial watercourse.

The extent of the easement prescribed for is determined by the extent of the user over the prescription period. The user which originates the right is also its measure (*Crossley and Sons Ltd v Lightowler* (1867) 2 Ch App 478, per Lord Chelmsford LC, at 481). If the claimant cannot clearly formulate the extent of his claim, but can only show a wide variation in the extent of his user over the alleged prescription period, he will fail (*Hulley v Silversprings Bleaching and Dyeing Co Ltd* [1922] 2 Ch 268). Where a prescriptive claim has been established but the user has later been varied it is a question of construction in every case whether there has been excessive user which can be prevented. In *Baxendale v McMurray* (1867) 2 Ch App 790, a person with a prescriptive right to pollute a stream with foul water from rag washings at his paper mill was held entitled to go on polluting with the washings from a new vegetable fibre as this was in the reasonable and proper course of his process of manufacture, providing the pollution did not substantially increase. But a right to discharge water into a stream will not usually include the right to discharge polluted water; such a right must be expressly proved if it is alleged to exist (*Cawkwell v Russell* (1856) 26 LJ Ex 34). No right to pollute to an extent dangerous to public health can be prescribed for because such a right could not lie in express grant or be presumed to be intended (*Blackburne v Somers* (1879) 5 LR Ir 1). If a person has a right of drainage for clean water and sends down foul water, the whole right of drainage may be stopped by the servient owner, since he cannot separate the clean water from the polluted water (*Cawkwell v Russell*). If a user has been pre-scribed for to do something at a particular time and place, it may be an excessive user to do the permitted thing at another time and place. In *McIntyre Brothers v McGavin* [1893] AC 268 the plaintiffs had a prescriptive right to take water from a stream at a certain place at their works and pollute it in their works, later returning it to the stream. This they could do at weekends. They claimed to take it at a spot a quarter of a mile below their works, at another time of the week, but were unsuccessful.

A riparian owner has no power to object to an alteration in the depth of the water adjacent to his land if it does not threaten to cause damage to his land or interfere with his acknowledged riparian rights or cause a nuisance to the occupier of the land (*Tate & Lyle Industries Ltd v Greater London Council* [1983] 2 WLR 649 (HL)).

There has been a right in the nature of an easement recognised by the courts in cases where, although there has been insufficient enjoyment to establish a prescriptive right, the servient owner has allowed the dominant owner to alter his position as if he had an easement and it would be inequitable to allow the servient owner subsequently to deny the right. In *Rochdale Canal Co v King* (1853) 16 Beav 630, a mill was built in 1830 close to the canal and pipes were laid, under the supervision of the canal company's officials, from the canal to the mill. The mill-owners used the water for many purposes known to the canal company but after a user of eighteen years the company unsuccessfully tried to forbid the use. The court said that if a man stands by and encourages another to lay out money under the expectation that no objection will subsequently be raised, the law will not allow him then to interfere with the enjoyment permitted. By contrast, in *Bankart v Tennant* (1870) LR 10 Eq 141, an understanding that the owners of a copper-works could use water from a canal so long as they were good customers of the canal company was held to give rise to no equitable obligation on the canal company to go on permitting the extraction of water. A person entitled to the benefit of an equitable right of this nature is not in as good a position as a person with a legal easement or with an equitable easement capable of subsisting as a legal interest. He cannot have specific performance to grant him a legal easement. He probably cannot register his right under the Land Charges Act 1972, s 2, as an equitable easement as he has not a positive right but only a valid defence to an assertion that he has no right (*Gale on Easements*, 15th ed, p 80, considers that he can register as an estate contract). The right may be enforceable against a successor in title of the grantor if its existence must have been patent and obvious to him (*Hervey v Smith* (1856) 22 Beav 299: right to use two chimneys in adjoining house), provided that the effect of the Land Charges Act 1972 is not to render actual notice irrelevant and to put all notice on the basis of registration. A dictum of Harman J, in *Hollington Brothers Ltd v Rhodes* [1951] 2 All ER 578, at 580, suggests that notice can only be by registration; *Emmet on Title*, 19th ed, para 5.144 agrees and discusses the matter fully. Non-registration is not fatal to enforcement where adjoining owners grant rights mutually to each other (*E R Ives Investments Ltd v High* [1967] 2 QB 379 (CA)). Non-registration might not be fatal if it would be a fraud for a claimant to rely on non-compliance with statute, *Lyus v Prowsa Developments Ltd* [1982] 1 WLR 1044, *Peffer v Rigg* [1977] 1 WLR 285.

The Law Reform Committee was asked by the Lord Chancellor in 1963 to consider the law relating to the acquisition of easements and profits by prescription. The report of the Committee (14th Report, Cmnd 3100), issued in October 1966, discloses a wide divergence of opinion on what form amendment of the law should take. Eight members of the Committee recommended the complete abolition of the right to acquire easements by prescription; the remaining six members recommended that easements should be capable of being acquired by a period of 12 years' prescriptive enjoyment (para 41), but that a system of notional interruption of enjoyment should be introduced (para 64). The Committee suggested unanimously that the Lands Tribunal should be empowered to discharge easements and also to substitute easements in a different place or of a different nature to secure the more efficient use of the servient land where the existence of the easement is preventing it, subject to a right to compensation to the dominant owner (para 97). No legislation has resulted.

The Law Reform Committee's Report was reviewed by the author at (1967) *Modern Law Review,* vol 30, p 189.

4 Ownership of the pipe

Where a pipe is laid in the land of another and enjoyed exclusively by the dominant owner by virtue of an easement, who owns the pipe? If it is laid under a written agreement which expressly states who is the owner, that will settle the question. If there is no such document the general law will apply. In *Simmons v Midford* [1969] 2 Ch 415 Buckley LJ, in discussing the legal maxim that whatever is in the soil is part of the soil, said that it concerned things which were previously chattels but had become physically attached to realty. In such a case the chattel may:

(a) lose its character as a chattel and adhere to the realty so as to become part of it for all purposes; or

(b) adhere to the realty whilst remaining a chattel so that the owner may subsequently detach it and re-possess it; or

(c) never lose its character as a chattel.

The facts of the case must be examined to see which of the three solutions is appropriate. In *Goodhart v Hyett* (1884) 25 ChD 182, where apparently the dominant owner had exclusive use of a conduit through the servient land, he was said by North J (at 186) to own the conduit. It is suggested that ownership of the pipe usually remains in the person who laid it: *Pemsel and Wilson v Tucker* [1907] 2 Ch 191 indirectly supports this proposition. Where a company had constructed a tunnel in adjoining land and had enjoyed the exclusive use of it, it was held that the company owned the tunnel itself and not a mere easement in the servient land (*Bevan v London Portland Cement Co Ltd* (1892) 67 LT 615). The case, therefore, goes beyond the enquiry whether a person who has an easement owns the pipe.

It was held in an old case, *Nicholas v Chamberlain* (1606) Cro Jac 121, that where a man had a house supplied by pipes and he sold off the house without the land through which the pipes came, the pipes would pass on the conveyance of the house: the case also says that if he kept the house and sold the land the pipes would go with the house, but the rule in *Wheeldon v Burrows* (1879) 12 ChD 31 would now prevent this unless the pipes were expressly reserved or the house owner could show an easement of necessity (*Gayford v Moffatt* (1868) 4 Ch App 133).

The dominant owner has an implied right to enter on the servient land to repair the pipe (*Pomfret v Ricroft* (1669) 1 Wms Saund (6th ed) 321, at 323) and can effectively be under a duty to do so, for he has no easement to have a leaking pipe on the servient land. Even if the dominant owner is not obliged to repair, he is liable for trespass or nuisance caused by an escape from the pipe and must therefore keep it watertight to avoid a trespass, *Ingram v Morecraft* (1863) 33 Beav 49, Lord Mansfield at 51, 52, *Jones v Pritchard* [1908] 1 Ch 638, Parker J. The position appears to be the same even if the servient owner also uses the pipe and could himself repair, *Buckley (R H) & Sons Ltd v Buckley (N) and Sons* [1898] 2 QB 608.

Apart from a requirement by statute, contract or custom there is no obligation on the servient owner to make repairs on his land to preserve the enjoyment of the easement (*Bond v Nottingham Corporation* [1940] Ch 429) but if a defect on the servient tenement amounts to a nuisance the servient owner is liable to the dominant owner if he does not take reasonable steps to abate it: *Leakey v National Trust* [1980] QB 485 (CA) (landslip); *Bradburn v Lindsay* [1983] 2 All ER 408 (dry rot and disrepair). In *Duke of Westminster v Guild* [1984] 3 All ER 144 (CA) it was held that where a lease made provision for a drain running under the property of both the tenant and the landlords to be repaired there was no need to imply a covenant to repair on the part of the landlords. Neither the express covenant for quiet enjoyment nor the implied covenant for non-derogation from grant could impose on the landlords positive obligations which they would not otherwise have.

Where there is no written agreement and the dominant and servient owners use the pipe jointly it is suggested that the servient owner will own the pipe to the extent that it runs under his land and that he will be entitled to a contribution to the cost of repair from the dominant owner proportionate to the dominant owner's use. Neither must use the pipe in such a manner as to prevent the other from doing so. If the pipe is fractured or blocked solely by the use to which one party puts it he will be solely responsible for repair.

In *Lee v Stevenson* (1858) EB & E 512, it was held that where a person granted to an adjoining owner the right to make a sewer in the former's land he could not then join his own sewer to it and use it. The court held that the dominant owner had the exclusive use of the sewer, 'a sewer of his own' (Crompton CJ, at 518). But it is not clear whether he meant that the dominant owner owned the pipe. In *Simmons v Midford* [1969] 2 Ch 415 it was held on the facts that a dominant owner there owned and had the exclusive right to use a pipe under the servient owner's land.

Where the pipe is laid in the land of another by licence, and there is no agreement as to ownership, the pipe will be regarded as part of the realty and will belong to the owner of the land through which it runs (*Armstrong v Sheppard & Short Ltd* [1959] 2 QB 384 (CA) per Lord Evershed MR at 401).

Even though a person may own the pipe which runs through another's land, he will not own any of the soil surrounding it. His right of occupation of the land only extends to the cavity which his pipe occupies and not to any of the surrounding or supporting soil (*Newcastle-under-Lyme Corporation v Wolstanton Ltd* [1947] Ch 427). He may have ancillary to his pipe easement a right of support and protection from the servient land (ibid).

Because of the current emphasis on environmental protection, it is particularly important that an agreement which permits the stationing of such things as pipes, cables or wires in or over the land of another, should also make provision for their removal by the layer or its successor. If they are left in the land and degrade, harmful materials may be produced. The landowner might then be liable to clean up, on the basis that 'polluter pays'.

5 Repair obligations

A dominant owner, though he is not bound to keep the subject of his easement in repair (*Taylor v Whitehead* (1781) 2 Doug KB 745) will be liable, if, for example, water escapes from his water-pipe running over another's land (*Ingram v Morecraft* (1863) 33 Beav 49, 51, 52; Parker J in *Jones v Pritchard* [1908] 1 Ch 638).

A servient owner is not bound to make repairs to ensure the continued enjoyment of the easement by the dominant owner. It appears from *Saint v Jenner* [1973] Ch 275 (CA) that if the servient owner disturbs the subject-matter of the easement (in this case by putting 'humps' onto a road across the land in order to slow down traffic, causing the road surface to deteriorate) he may be liable in nuisance to the dominant owner whose enjoyment of the easement is interfered with. The case could be regarded as an example of derogation from grant (in reverse). If the dominant owner covenants to pay a contribution to repair of the way and does not do so, *Gale* (15th ed) p 48 suggests that it is an open question whether his right to use determines on his default or is merely suspended until he makes his contribution (citing *Duncan v Louch* (1845) 6 QB 904 per curiam). *Gale* also suggests that the stipulation as to contribution is a covenant which could be enforced against the original grantee by the servient owner for the time being.

Chapter 4

Termination of the Easement

1 Termination by statute

An easement may be brought to an end expressly by statute. For example, under the Town and Country Planning Act 1990, s 236 on the compulsory acquisition of land by the acquiring authority 'all private rights of way and rights of laying down, erecting, continuing or maintaining any apparatus on, under or over the land shall be extinguished, and any such apparatus shall vest in the acquiring authority' (s 236(1)). A right to compensation is given by s 236(4) to the person who suffers loss by the extinguishment. A right to lay and use pipes, cables and drains would be covered by this section. By s 236(2), subs (1) does not apply 'to any right vested in, or apparatus belonging to, statutory undertakers for the purpose of the carrying on of their undertaking'.

An easement may also be extinguished by statute by implication, where its continued existence would conflict with the carrying out of the thing authorised by the statute. In *Yarmouth Corporation v Simmons* (1878) 10 ChD 518 there was statutory authority to make a pier, but a public right of way would have prevented this being done. It was held that the statute by implication extinguished the way. Similar cases might easily arise affecting pipes and drains. But it is suggested that the easement will only be extinguished by implication if its destruction is a necessary inference from the words used by the statute (*Shonleigh Nominees Ltd v AG* [1974] 1 WLR 305 (HL)). In any particular case the court may find that the easement continues. In *Bond v Nottingham Corporation* [1940] Ch 429 the servient tenement was compulsorily demolished under the (then) Housing Act 1936, but it was held that the local authority must supply to the dominant tenement an equivalent support in substitution for the support formerly supplied by the servient tenement, the dominant owner having an easement. In *Walsh v Oates* [1953] 1 QB 578 (CA) an order for stopping up a highway under the Highway Act 1835 was held to extinguish a public right of way over the road but not a private way over it. In *Mann v R C Eayrs Ltd* (1973) 231 EG 843, a person had a right of way over some land. The Air Ministry requisitioned the land and forbade him to use the way but they provided another way for him. After the requisitioning ended it was held that he had not lost the right to use again the first way but he had not acquired a prescriptive right to use the second way.

If a person has a private easement over servient land and acquires the same easement by statute, the private easement will merge in the statutory one. So, if the grant by statute is for a limited period only, after that period the private one will not continue (*New Windsor Corporation v Taylor* [1899] AC 41).

Where a person's easement is extinguished by statute he should be advised to consider whether the statute expressly or impliedly entitles him to compensation, for example, under the Lands Clauses Consolidation Act 1845 (*Hill v Midland Railway Co* (1882) 21 ChD 143). The courts will not assume that private rights are intended by Parliament to be removed without compensation, for that is simply confiscation (*Wells v London, Tilbury and Southend Railway Co* (1877) 5 ChD 126, per Bramwell LJ, at 130).

2 Termination by express agreement

Since a legal easement is a legal interest in land (Law of Property Act 1925, s 1(2)(a)), and a release of the servient owner from it by a dominant owner operates as a conveyance of a legal interest (s 205(1)), the release must be by deed (s 52). A purported release not under seal may still be of evidential value if it can be coupled with acts of cessation of user to show intention to relinquish the easement. If the strict formalities of release have not been complied with but one party has been induced to alter his position or to lay out money on the basis that there is a valid release, so that it would be inequitable for the person inducing the belief to rely on the informality, he will be restrained from doing so (*Poulton v Moore* [1915] 1 KB 400). Similarly, a verbal permission to do some act which will destroy or alter the easement cannot be resiled from by the person giving it, after it has been acted on (*Liggins v Inge* (1831) 7 Bing 682). For example, if the dominant owner authorises the servient owner to take up a drain and redevelop the servient land he cannot, in the absence of a prior agreement to that effect, claim to have the drain restored later when the redevelopment has been carried out, even though he had an enforceable easement of drainage before. He should, prudently, make a variation by deed with a fresh right of drainage in the new scheme.

The releasing party cannot release an easement to a greater extent than his own interest in the dominant tenement. For example, a tenant for life of the dominant tenement can, under the Settled Land Act 1925, s 58, release the servient land completely from an easement if he has the consent in writing of the trustees of the settlement. If he has not this consent, he can release it for his own lifetime only and it would again be exercisable after his death (see *Davis v Morgan* (1825) 4 B & C 8). There appears to be no decision on the question whether a valid release can be made by a competent releasor to a releasee who has only a limited interest in the servient land. If *A*, who owns the fee simple of the dominant land, which is entitled to a water supply through the servient land, makes a deed with *B*, the tenant for life of the servient land, releasing him and the land from the easement, can *A* re-assert his claim when *B*'s interest ends? It is suggested that *A*'s release might be taken as evidence of abandonment and found to be effective on that score.

3 Termination by unity of seisin

If one person becomes both the dominant and servient owner for the same estate or interest in each tenement then the easements formerly enjoyed by him in the servient land will be extinguished. He henceforth enjoys both lands by virtue of his ownership; he cannot have anything in the nature of a right against himself over his own land (*Kilgour v Gaddes* [1904] 1 KB 457). If he subsequently sells off one tenement, in the absence of express agreement the rule in *Wheeldon v Burrows* (1879) 12 ChD 31 and the Law of Property Act 1925, s 62 will apply. He will not at common law be entitled to an easement over the land sold off unless he expressly reserves it.

If one person acquires both tenements for other than identical estates the easement will be suspended during his tenure of both and will continue upon termination of his joint holding. For example, in *Simper v Foley* (1862) 2 J & H 555, the dominant owner in fee simple acquired a lease in the servient land. Later he disposed of the lease and it was held that after disposal he could continue to enjoy an easement over the servient land which he had enjoyed before he took the lease.

Where a person obtains unity of seisin but not unity of possession, for example, where he acquires the fee simple of the servient land and the freehold reversion only of the dominant land because it is subject to a lease, it is not decided whether there is extinguishment of easements or not (*Buckby v Coles* (1814) 5 Taunt 311, at 315). It is suggested that whilst the lease continues there can be no extinguishment of any rights which the leaseholder has against the servient land, that the reversioner, not being in possession, cannot use any easements and that once the lease terminates the easements must be extinguished by reason of the unity of seisin. Where a person has unity of possession but not unity of seisin (such as where he obtains a lease of both tenements) all easements existing before such unity will be exercisable after it terminates (*Canham v Fisk* (1831) 2 C & J 126).

It may be important to distinguish an easement from a natural right of ownership. If a dominant owner in fee simple acquires a servient tenement in fee simple over which he had previously enjoyed a right of drainage through a pipe, then unity of seisin will destroy his easement, and if he subsequently sells off the former servient land without expressly stipulating for his drainage he cannot claim that the easement revives for his benefit. His only course would be to establish an easement of necessity. If, on the other hand, he acquired the servient land through which a natural stream flowed from the dominant land he would not, after severance, need to show any easement to have the flow of the stream continued. If the servient owner extracted the water for purposes unconnected with his riparian ownership the dominant owner could prevent this by virtue of his natural rights as a riparian owner (*Portsmouth Borough Waterworks Co v London, Brighton, and South Coast Railway Co* (1909–10) 26 TLR 173).

A person may own both dominant and servient tenements but in different capacities. For example, a clergyman may have the church vested in him as trustee and the adjoining glebe lands vested in him as beneficial owner (*Ecclesiastical Commissioners for England v Kino* (1880) 14 Ch D 213). In this case it was held that the easements continued just as if there were separate owners.

4 Termination by implication

An easement will be regarded as terminated if circumstances can be found which indicate an intention on the part of the dominant owner from which a release or abandonment can be implied. In *Tehidy Minerals Ltd v Norman* [1971] 2 QB 182 (CA) it was held that abandonment of an easement or profit à prendre can only be treated as taking place when the person entitled to it has demonstrated a fixed intention never at any time thereafter to assert the right himself or attempt to transmit it to anyone else. In *Williams v Usherwood* (1983) 45 P & CR 235 (CA) it was held that an easement is abandoned if the owner of it makes it clear that he has a firm intention that neither he nor any successor in title should thereafter make use of it (adopting the words of Buckley LJ in *Gotobed v Pridmore* (1970) 115 SJ 78). The various circumstances are categorised below.

Ceasing to use the easement

Mere non-user of an easement will not of itself amount to abandonment. For example, a person with a right to a supply of water from another's land may cease to use the water because he has sold the cattle he used to need it for, but he may intend to buy some more next year and will then resume the use; again a person may not exercise his right of eavesdrop, because no rain has fallen recently, but he will use the right when the rain falls again. To constitute a case of termination by non-user there must be other circumstances besides non-exercise (*Ward v Ward* (1852) 7 Ex 838); 'the non-user must be the consequence of something which is adverse to the user' (Alderson B, at 839). The question of whether the easement has been abandoned is a question of fact in each case. Non-user may be explicable because, for example, an artificial stream previously enjoyed changed its course for some years and then returned to its old course, whereupon enjoyment recommenced. In such a case it may be held that there had been no abandonment (see *Hall v Swift* (1838) 4 Bing (NC) 381, a case concerning a natural watercourse). Non-user where the dominant owner has been forbidden to use the easement on requisitioning of the servient land is not evidence of abandonment of the easement (*Mann v RC Eayrs Ltd* (1973) 231 EG 843; *Tehidy Minerals Ltd v Norman* [1971] 2 QB 183 (CA); *Re Yateley Common, Hampshire* [1977] 1 WLR 840). But failure to exercise the right for a long period may place the dominant owner under the obligation of showing how, during his non-exercise, he gave evidence of his continued claim to the right. In a case where a dye-works had a right to pollute a stream but the works had been demolished, a person who claimed to recommence the pollution 25 years later under the same right was unsuccessful (*Crossley and Sons Ltd v Lightowler* (1867) LR 3 Eq 279). It is not so much the period of cesser as the nature of the adverse act and the intention which it indicates which are to be considered (*Hale v Oldroyd* (1845) 14 M & W 789).

There is no rule of law that non-user for any particular time must amount to abandonment comparable to the rule that an easement may be acquired by prescription after enjoyment for a fixed period. In *Ward v Ward*, above, an easement was held not to have been abandoned though it was not enjoyed during a period of about 38 years, and in *Cook v Bath Corporation* (1868) LR 6 Eq 177, a non-user for 40 years did not amount to an abandonment. It was said in *R v Chorley* (1848) 12 QB 515, that where non-user or an acquiescence in obstruction were relied on as evidence of abandonment it would not be prudent to accept a period of less than 20 years' non-user or acquiescence. So for practical purposes a minimum of 20 years must be shown, but there is no fixed maximum. Indeed, in *Benn v Hardinge* (1992) 66 P & CR 246 (CA) it was held that non-user of a way for 175 years, during which time it became entirely grown-over, did not amount to abandonment, in the absence of evidence of intention to abandon.

Although non-user of an easement does not effect, or give rise to a presumption of, abandonment (*Gotobed v Pridmore* (1970) 217 EG 759) yet an easement created by express grant is capable of being partially released or extinguished by deed or by implication; *Snell & Prideaux Ltd v Dutton Mirrors Ltd* [1994] EGCS 78 (CA) (servient owner built over part of a right of way, dominant owner objected some 30 years later. Held: damages were an adequate remedy, as the court would be slow to infer from non-objection that the right had been abandoned totally. Damages would reflect the reduced rights of access now to be enjoyed).

If a person loses his land because of the adverse possession of another he will lose also any easements which he enjoys by virtue of his owning that land. In *Williams v Usherwood* (1983) 45 P & CR 235 (CA) the owners of two adjoining houses each owned a share of the joint driveway and had an easement of way over the other's part. By various acts of ownership of one owner and inactivity on the part of the other the first gained a title to part of the drive of the second by adverse possession. It followed that the second lost his easement of way over the drive of the first. He did not however lose the entitlement to use the drains under his 'lost' drive as there had been no adverse act against this user.

A user of the easement in part only will not prejudice any future claim by the dominant owner to resume a full use (*Keewatin Power Co Ltd v Lake of the Woods Milling Co Ltd* [1930] AC 640, per Viscount Dunedin, at 657).

Altering dominant tenement or altering burden on servient tenement

Where a person alters the dominant tenement so as in effect to enjoy a different easement from the one he has acquired, or alters his user so that he brings about the same result, it is a question of construction in every case whether he has evinced an intention to abandon the easement (in which case he cannot subsequently resume the enjoyment of it) or whether he has simply made an excessive user (which can be forbidden without affecting his right to enjoy the original easement).

Mere increase in user will not usually amount to excessive user, as is shown by *British Railways Board v Glass* [1965] Ch 538 (increased user of land by caravans); *Woodhouse & Co Ltd v Kirkland Ltd* [1970] 1 WLR 1185 (increased user of way by dominant owners' customers); and *Cargill v Gotts* [1981] 1 WLR 441 (CA) (greatly increased abstraction of water because of new methods of irrigation by crop-spraying).

A person who materially altered the dominant tenement or the user would in effect be prescribing for a new easement. In *Cargill v Gotts* (above) Lawton LJ suggested that if part of the farm had been turned into a trout hatchery the use of water for that purpose might be outside the prescriptive easement already acquired to take water for farm purposes generally.

If a person owns a house which is drained through another's land and he demolishes the house, intending to make an allotment of the land, he cannot subsequently build another house and claim his former easement (*Liggins v Inge* (1831) 7 Bing 682). The case would be otherwise if he demolished with a view to reconstruction. The easement will be extinguished if there is evidence from the circumstances of intention to relinquish it, though the non-user may not have lasted 20 years (*Moore v Rawson* (1824) 3 B & C 332, at 341).

If the dominant tenement is not demolished but merely altered, the intention to relinquish is harder to find. Not every alteration in the dominant tenement will increase the burden on the servient. In *Thomas v Thomas* (1835) 2 Cr M & R 34, a person had a right to eavesdrop from pantiles on his building onto neighbouring land. The building caught fire and was repaired with thatch which projected over the neighbour's land four inches more than the pantiles had done: the wall of the building was also raised about three feet. It was held that the alterations in no way affected the easement. A person with a right to a supply of water to his house who has a bath put in for the first time will probably not use so much more water than he did before as to make any appreciable increase in burden. A changed user which does not materially increase the burden cannot be evidence of an intention to abandon the former easement. But if the person entitled to the water supply added a public car-wash to his house he might require so much more water as to amount to an abandonment of his right to have a domestic supply. If the excessive user complained of is severable from the permitted user the easement will not be lost by the dominant owner, but if no severance is possible he may be held to have abandoned his easement. For example, if a person with a right to drain rainwater through a pipe drains foul water through it continuously he can be forbidden to use it at all, for the clean water cannot be separated from the foul water (*Cawkwell v Russell* (1856) 26 LJ Ex 34). If a person 'adds on' another dominant tenement to the one which the easement was granted to serve he may be liable for excessive user. In *Bracewell v Appleby* [1975] Ch 408 a person with a right of way to plot *A* acquired plot *B* behind it and built a house there. It was held that he had no right to use the way to go to plot *B*, but an injunction to forbid him from doing so was refused and damages were awarded instead. To have granted an injunction would have made the house on plot *B* unusable. (The correctness of this refusal was doubted in *Anchor Brewhouse Developments Ltd v Berkeley House (Docklands Developments) Ltd* [1987] 2 EGLR 173.) If a person adopts a different user completely from the one he had an easement for, then he can be restrained from his new user even though it does not impose a greater burden on the servient land than the old one did. Excessive user becomes irrelevant if he has no right to the new use: *Clarke v Somersetshire Drainage Commissioners* (1888) 59 LT 670 (right to pour into a stream the washings from a fellmongery: new business of leather-board manufacturers commenced: held, that there was no right to pour into the stream the foul washings from this even though they were no more foul than the others had been).

If a person loses his dominant tenement because of adverse possession of it by the servient owner he will lose also the easement which the dominant tenement enjoys over the servient land. He may, however, retain an easement over the land and thereby lose his dominant tenement if there has been no adverse act towards the easement (drainage retained, way lost in *Williams v Usherwood* (1983) 45 P & CR 235 (CA); similarly *Marshall v Taylor* [1895] 1 Ch 641 (CA)).

One dominant owner cannot sue another dominant owner for interference by excessive user with an easement which they both enjoy unless the user substantially obstructs his own enjoyment; if one causes pot-holes in a road used by both this alone will not found an action (*Weston v Lawrence Weaver Ltd* [1961] 1 QB 402), and it cannot be construed as an abandonment of his easement by the offender.

In the absence of agreement one dominant owner is not under an obligation to repair the land the subject of the easement. If he fails to repair he may harm himself by making the exercise of his easement more difficult or even impossible, as where he allows a drain to silt up, or he may provide evidence from which abandonment of the easement can be inferred. A dominant owner is liable for his failure to repair if by so failing he comes to exercise a right different from that granted or prescribed for. For example, if he fails to repair his pipe so that it leaks onto the servient owner's land he now exercises a right to run a leaking pipe over the land, which was not the original right (*Jones v Pritchard* [1908] 1 Ch 630, Parker J, at 638). The dominant owner can go onto the servient land so as to repair it to allow continued use of the easement but if he goes beyond repair he may afford himself evidence of ownership (*Williams v Usherwood* (1983) 45 P & CR 235).

The owner of the servient land is not under a duty to repair so as to enable continued enjoyment of the easement (*Bond v Nottingham Corporation* (1940) Ch 429) but if the neglect of the servient land amounts to a nuisance the servient owner will be liable (*Bradburn v Lindsay* [1983] 2 All ER 408).

5 Termination for impossibility of exercise

It was held in *Huckvale v Aegean Hotels Ltd* (1989) 58 P & CR 163 (CA) that whilst it might be possible for an easement to be extinguished where circumstances were such that there was no longer any practical possibility of it ever again benefiting the dominant tenement in the manner contemplated by the grant which created it, the question of whether that had occurred was a matter of fact and degree in each case. The mere lack of current practical use was far from extinguishment.

There may be a principle that in the case of a way of necessity the right to use the way will cease when the necessity ends; *Holmes v Goring* (1824) 2 Bing 76, but Nourse LJ in the *Huckvale case* thought that the observation of Best CJ on the point in *Holmes* was possibly obiter.

6 Consequences of termination

Where an easement terminates, it can be important to the servient owner that the pipe, cable, sewer or other thing is removed. If the termination is by agreement with the dominant owner, it should be stipulated who effects the removal. If termination is by acquiescence or other cause, the servient owner should attend to removal in case the pipe degrades and releases toxic materials. The owner could then be liable under the 'polluter pays' principle of current environmental legislation. In addition, an undisclosed pipe could be held to be a defect in title which should be disclosed on a sale of the land, as in *William Sindall plc v Cambridgeshire County Council* [1994] 1 WLR 1016 (CA) (disused sewer).

7 Non-existence of easement

It is important not to misdescribe property. In *Dodd v Crown Estate Commissioners* [1995] EGCS 35 the plan annexed to agents' particulars showed a drain from property going into the main drain. The conveyance was made. The buyer found that there was no main drain and the seller was unable to grant drainage rights into the main drain. The seller was liable for all losses which flowed from the innocent misrepresentation, foreseeable or not, provided they were not too remote (*Royscot Trust v Rogerson* [1991] 3 WLR 57 (CA)).

Part II

Pipes Laid under Statutory Powers

Chapter 5

Statutory Bodies and Compulsory Acquisition

1 Statutory bodies

Statutory bodies are created by statute and derive their powers from statute. They are corporate bodies. For example, the Local Government Act 1972 ('1972 Act') set up county councils and district councils to be the local authorities to replace urban district, rural district, parish and county councils under the Local Government Act 1933 (1972 Act, ss 2, 270). The Water Act 1973 ('1973 Act') set up regional water authorities to be responsible for (inter alia) the supply of water (s 11), for sewerage and sewage disposal (s 14), for the prevention of pollution of rivers and coastal waters (s 9), and for supervising land drainage (s 19). (They were replaced by the Water Act 1989 and Water Industry Act 1991.) The Gas Act 1986 (ss 49, 57) provided that the property and rights of the British Gas Corporation were to vest in a new company, British Gas plc.

An authority cannot act otherwise than in accordance with its powers; it must not act without powers and it must not exceed those powers it has (*AG v Fulham Corporation* [1921] 1 Ch 440). The powers may be either directly conferred by an Act or capable of derivation by reasonable implication from its provisions (*Baroness Wenlock v River Dee Co* (1885) 10 App Cas 354, at 362–3), or capable of being regarded as reasonably incidental to something for which there is express or implied authority (*AG v Great Eastern Railway Co* (1880) 5 App Cas 472, at 478; 1972 Act, s 111). The powers of an authority are either compulsory or adoptive. A sewerage undertaker must, for example, provide such public sewers as may be necessary for effectually draining the area (Water Industry Act 1991, s 94). By contrast, a relevant undertaker

75

has power, for carrying out its functions, to lay a pipe in, over or under any street (s 158(1)).

2 Compulsory acquisition

Where an authority has power to acquire land by agreement or compulsorily a standard procedure governs the transaction. The procedure is laid down in the Acquisition of Land Act 1981 and the Compulsory Purchase Act 1965. Persons affected must be notified and advertisement is made in a local newspaper. If there are objections a local enquiry may be held.

If agreement is not reached between the parties compensation is assessed by the Lands Tribunal, under the Land Compensation Acts 1961 and 1973. Relevant considerations are not only the type of land taken and its location but also any reduction in the value of the land retained by the owner by reason of its severance from the land compulsorily taken (Compulsory Purchase Act 1965, s 7). Compensation is also payable where land has been injuriously affected by the taking of land nearby, even though none of the land affected has been taken (Lands Clauses Consolidation Act 1845, s 68; Compulsory Purchase Act 1965, s 10). The classes of 'blighted land' in respect of which a claim for compensation can be made have been extended by Pt V of the Land Compensation Act 1973. Not only the actual use but also the prospective use of the land had the order not been made is relevant in assessing compensation for severance (*R v Brown* (1867) LR 2 QB 630: agricultural land rendered unsuitable for building in future). The provisions of the Land Compensation Act 1961, Pt II, ss 5–16, must be applied in assessing the compensation. Section 5 of this Act sets out the following rules for assessment:

(a) No allowance shall be made for the fact that the purchase was compulsory.

(b) The land shall be valued on an open market basis as if the sale were by a willing seller.

(c) The special suitability of the land for a particular purpose shall be ignored if that purpose is one to which it could only have been applied under statutory powers or for which there is no market apart from the special needs of the compulsory purchaser.

(d) If the land is used in a manner contrary to law or injurious to health and by that use its value is increased, the increase is disregarded.

(e) Where land is used for a purpose for which there is no general demand (such as a church) compensation is assessed on the basis of the cost of equivalent reinstatement elsewhere. In *Birmingham Corporation v West Midland Baptist (Trust) Association Inc* [1970] AC 874 it was held that the compensation is assessed as at the date when the reinstatement might reasonably have commenced and not at the earlier date when the notice to treat was served.

(f) Compensation for disturbance or any other matter not directly related to the value of the land is unaffected by the provisions of rule *(b)* above.

These six rules must be read in conjunction with ss 7 and 10 of the Compulsory Purchase Act 1965 and Pt IV of the Land Compensation Act 1973.

The fact that a very large award of compensation is made in respect of a small area of land cannot be objected to by the buyer if the award is made on a correct application of the relevant law. In *Ward Construction (Medway) Ltd v Barclays Bank* (1994) *The Times,* 20 July (CA) (following *Stokes v Cambridge Corporation* (1961) 13 P & CR 77) an award of £2.15 million for 0.86 acre of land (needed to complete an off-site road for a large development) was made. This was not a case within the rule in *Pointe-Gourde Quarrying & Transport Co Ltd v Sub-Intendent of Crown Lands* [1947] AC 565 where the increase in value was entirely due to the scheme underlying the acquisition (see rule *(c)* above).

By s 37(1) of the Land Compensation Act 1973 where a person is displaced from land by a compulsory acquisition he is entitled to a disturbance payment, and by s 38(1) the amount is to be equal to *(a)* his reasonable expenses of moving and *(b)* the loss he will suffer because his trade or business on the land is disturbed. It was held in *Prasad v Wolverhampton Borough Council* [1983] 2 All ER 140 (CA) that the loss does not have to follow the dispossession in time; it can be loss incurred by the owner in making arrangements when he knew that acquisition was inevitable. The only requirement was that the claimant must establish that the loss was connected to the acquisition. Thus he may claim the expenses if he moves to other accommodation even before he is given notice to treat. *Prasad* was followed in *Sheffield Development Corporation v Glossop Sectional Buildings Ltd* [1994] 1 WLR 1676 (CA) (company which ceased to trade before being required compulsorily to give up possession of its land and retained a compensatable interest in it).

Regulations govern the procedure and the forms used on compulsory purchase (see the Compulsory Purchase of Land Regulations 1994 (SI No 2145)), and vary the rates of interest payable after entry on the land (see the current Acquisition of Land (Rate of Interest after Entry) Regulations). The Department of the Environment issues circulars on aspects of compulsory acquisition; for example, on the Award of Costs incurred in Planning and other (including Compulsory Purchase Orders) Proceedings (No 8 of 1993); and Compulsory Purchase Orders: Procedures (No 14/ 1994). The circulars may be found in the *Encyclopaedia of Compulsory Purchase and Compensation* (Sweet & Maxwell), Vol 2, part IV.

Chapter 6

Water Supply

From 1 April 1974, the responsibility for the public supply of water was transferred from local authorities to the water authority for the area (Water Act 1973, s 11). The 1973 Act set up nine regional water authorities in England and the Welsh National Water Development Authority (s 2, Sched 1). Statutory water companies could remain in existence and continue to supply water as agents for the water authorities (s 12). The constitution and procedure of water authorities was governed by s 3 of the 1973 Act (supplied by s 1 of the Water Act 1983).

The objects of the 1973 Act were to end the previous piecemeal treatment of the supply of water, and to provide for the disposal of polluted water and sewage, the use of inland waters for navigation and recreation, and the restoration of the wholesomeness of rivers, by vesting the powers and duties in respect of each matter in the hands of the one authority in each area (s 1). The powers of the water authority were increased by the Control of Pollution Act 1974.

The Water Act 1989 (in force from 1 December 1991) provided for the restructuring and privatisation of the water industry in England and Wales. The Act transferred the property, rights, and liabilities of the existing water authorities to a newly-established National Rivers Authority and then to private companies nominated by the Secretary of State. The water authorities were dissolved (ss 1, 3). Each water authority was required to make a scheme providing for the transfer of its undertaking to the National Rivers Authority after approval by the Secretary of State (Sched 2). However, the National Rivers Authority and the London Waste Regulation Authority were abolished by s 2(3) of the Environment Act 1995 and their property, rights and liabilities were transferred to the Environment Agency on the transfer date. This chapter should be read accordingly.

The legislation relating to water was consolidated in 1991 in the Water Industry Act ('WIA'), the Water Resources Act ('WRA'), the Statutory Water Companies Act, the Land Drainage Act and the Water Consolidation (Consequentional Provisions) Act, following the Law Commission Report 198 Cmnd 1483 (1991).

In the WRA the National Rivers Authority was continued by s 1 and its functions set out in s 2. There are duties under s 16 to further natural beauty and to ensure conservation. It continues the regional rivers advisory committees set up under the Water Act, s 2 (WRA, s 7). The Authority's functions include those of the former water authorities not assumed by water or sewerage undertakings (WIA, s 4(1)). The Director General of Water Services is continued, with customer service committees, each allocated to a water or sewerage undertaker (WIA, s 1(1)). The Secretary of State or the Director must exercise his or their powers in a manner considered to be best calculated to secure that the functions of water and sewerage undertakers are properly carried out and the interests of consumers are protected (WIA, s 2(3)). In formulating or considering any proposals the Secretary, the Minister, the Authority, the Director and any relevant body must take into account and have regard to conservation of the environment, protection of archeological sites and buildings of architectural or historic interest and the protection of recreational areas of beauty (WIA, ss 3–5). The Secretary of State may approve codes of practice with respect to environmental and recreational duties (WIA, s 5).

The National Rivers Authority and the Director-General of Water Services have regulatory and policing functions (WIA, s 2).

The Authority is responsible for conserving, redistributing or otherwise allocating water resources in England and Wales (WRA, s 19 and Pt II), for entering into water resources management schemes with water undertakers (WRA, s 20), for determining minimum acceptable river flows (WRA, s 21), for asking the Secretary of State (or the water undertaker may apply) to make drought orders (WRA, ss 78–81), for making arrangements about flood defence and establishing regional flood defence committees in place of regional land drainage committees (WRA, ss 9–14), for granting licences to abstract water (WRA, ss 34–72), and for control of pollution of water resources (WRA, ss 82–104). Water can be supplied by private undertakers, subject to supervision by local authorities; Private Water Supplies Regulations 1991 (SI 2790), Circular 68/91.

1 General duties of water undertakers

By WIA, s 37(1) it shall be the duty of every water undertaker to develop and maintain an efficient and economical system of water supply within its area and to ensure that arrangements are made for providing supplies of water to premises and to persons who demand them; and for maintaining, improving and extending the water undertaker's mains and other pipes. The duty is enforceable by the Secretary of State or the Director (WIA, s 37(2)). The Secretary may by regulations prescribe such standards of performance in connection with the provision of supplies in general or to individual consumers as in his opinion ought to be achieved in individual cases (WIA, s 38). Regulations have been made in respect of domestic consumers: Water Supply and Sewerage Services (Customer Service Standards) Regulations 1989 (SI No 1159) (amended by SI No 1383/89). The Director may order an undertaker to give a bulk supply to another undertaker (WIA, s 40).

The Competition and Service (Utilities) Act 1992 gives effect to a government commitment contained in the Citizen's Charter (HMSO, Cm 1599) to give the Directors General for water, gas, electricity and telecommunications further legal powers to ensure that better services are provided for consumers. For each utility the Act provides for the Directors to make regulations for standards of performance, to collect information on levels of performance and to make it available, to establish procedures for dealing with consumers' complaints and to determine disputes, including those on billing and (where relevant) to prevent disconnections in cases where there is a genuine dispute. This last provision will not apply where disputing the bill is a tactic to avoid payment, *Jones v East Ham Corporation* [1935] 1 KB 367.

2 Supplies through water mains

An owner or occupier of premises, a local authority in the undertaker's area, a new town authority, the Development Board for Rural Wales and an urban development corporation are all entitled to requisition the provision of a water main for any locality and the water undertaker is under a duty to supply it (WIA, s 41(1)) within three months of the date of a requisition (WIA, s 44(1)). The undertaker may impose financial conditions on the supplying of a main (WIA, s 42(1)). These conditions are based on the cost of funding the mains by means of a hypothetical loan of the capital required, over a 12 year period (WIA, ss 42, 43).

By s 45(4) any breach of the duty to supply which causes the requisitioner loss or damage is actionable by him but the defence of 'due diligence' and 'taking all reasonable steps' to avoid the breach is open to the water undertaker. A delay of 20 years in supplying 773 holiday chalets with water and sewers was held too long in *R v Secretary of State ex p Jaywick Sands Freeholders Association Ltd* (1975) JPL 663.

The Water Industry Act, ss 45–47 deal with the undertaker's duty to make a connection of a service pipe to the water mains. The owner or lawful occupier of land (but probably not a squatter, *Woodstock v South Western Electricity Board* [1975] 1 WLR 152) can serve notice on the undertaker requiring a supply of water for domestic purposes and the undertaker will be under a duty to connect at the expense of the person serving notice unless the main is neither a trunk main nor one which is used or to be used solely for the purpose of supplying water for non-domestic purposes (s 45(1), (2)). Any duty owed under s 45 is owed to the person who served the notice, s 42(2). The duty can include that of laying a service pipe in the street between the main and the applicant's property at the applicant's expense (s 46) and can be complied with by laying a main and not a service pipe (s 47). The undertaker may impose conditions on agreeing to comply with a notice, such as that financial security is provided for the expenses, that an approved meter is installed or that so much of a service pipe as is to be used by but has not been installed by the under-taker complies with approved specifications (s 47). The undertaker may require the provision of a separate service pipe to any prem-ises which consist of a house or other building or part of a building which is separately occupied and already supplied but does not have a separate service pipe (ss 47(2)(*e*), 50). The undertaker owes a 'domestic supply duty' in relation to any premises connected under s 45 or supplied before the transfer date from the water authority (s 52(1), (2)). The duty is to provide the premises with a supply of water sufficient for domestic purposes and to main-tain a connection between the main and the service pipe, but this is not to apply to a period when it would be reasonable for the water to be cut off or reduced for the purpose of carrying out any necessary works (WIA, ss 52(1), (7), 54).

The owner or occupier of premises can request a supply of water for non-domestic purposes but there will be no duty to supply him if to do so would require the undertaker to incur unreasonable expenditure (s 55). Every water authority at the request of the fire authority shall fix fire-hydrants on its water mains (other than trunk mains) at such places as may be most convenient for affording a supply of water for extinguishing fires in the area and the undertaker must keep the fire-hydrants in good working order (s 57). An undertaker shall supply at the request of a sewerage undertaker a supply of water for such purposes as cleansing sewers and drains, cleansing or watering highways or supplying any public pumps, baths or wash-houses (s 59) on such terms and conditions as may be reasonable (s 59(2)). The matter is policed by the Secretary of State or the Director (s 18).

By s 158 the undertaker has power to lay a 'relevant pipe', as defined in s (7) in streets and to inspect, maintain, adjust, repair or alter it and to carry out any works requisite for breaking up, or opening, tunnelling or boring, breaking or opening a sewer, drain or tunnel, or moving or removing earth or other materials. By s 159 the undertaker may lay pipes in land which is not in, under or over a street and keep the pipe there, inspecting and repairing as needed; necessary incidental work may also be carried out.

The 'premises' which are entitled to demand a supply of water from the authority need not be conventional structures: in *West Mersea Urban District Council v Fraser* [1950] 2 KB 119 a houseboat moored on a mud flat was held entitled to a supply. It is questionable whether a person who occupies premises as a trespasser is entitled to demand a supply. In *Woodstock v South Western Electricity Board* [1975] 1 WLR 152 it was held that a 'squatter' in premises was not entitled to demand a supply of electricity as he was not an 'owner or occupier' within the Electric Lighting (Clauses) Act 1899, Sched, s 27. Section 45 of the WIA uses the word 'owner'.

By WIA, s 142(1), (4) a relevant undertaker may fix charges for any services provided by reference to such matters and by such principles 'as appear to the undertaker to be appropriate'. By ss 142–150 the Director General of Water Services oversees the level of such charges. Both water and sewerage undertakers must comply with their instruments of appointment under WIA, s 6. In *Daymond v South West Water Authority* [1976] AC 609 it was held that a water rate was not payable by a person who is not connected to the water supply; now a reduced rate could be levied. A person who had no water supply to his shop premises but had a contractual right under his lease to use a communal lavatory a short distance away was held liable for a water rate under ss 38 and 59 of the 1945 Act in *West Pennine Water Board v Jon Migael (North West) Ltd* (1975) 73 LGR 420 (CA). In *South West Water Authority v Rumbles* [1985] 1 All ER 513 (HL) a shop had no water supply or connection to drainage but the roof on the shop premises drained into a sewer. As the shop had the use of the roof and its drainage facility it was liable for a sewerage charge. Section 59 defined 'premises' as including any interest in land and any easement or right in, to or over land.

An express planning permission is not required by the water authority for the laying underground of mains, pipes or other apparatus, as there is a general permission given by the Town and Country Planning General Development Order 1988 (SI No 1813), Sched 2, Pt 17, Class E.

3 New premises

Where a local authority is asked to approve the plans for new houses it must not do so unless they show satisfactory arrangements for the provision to them of a supply, sufficient for the domestic purposes of the occupants, of wholesome water from the water authority system, or (if this is not reasonably practicable) from some other piped supply, or (if this is not reasonably practicable) from a source within a reasonable distance of the premises (Building Act 1984, s 25(1)(2), (6)). If the plans are approved but they are not adhered to and a sufficient supply is not provided, the local authority may forbid occupation until the matter is put right (1984 Act, s 25(3)).

An owner of land who proposes to erect houses on it can make a water main requisition under WIA, s 41(1) that the water undertaker shall provide a water main to provide 'such supplies of water . . . as are sufficient for domestic purposes'. This is so even though the request may go beyond the undertaker's infrastructure plans under its general duty in s 37 to 'develop and maintain an efficient and economical system of water supply.' By ss 42 and 43 the requisitioner must satisfy financial requirements. There may be an issue about the route of the main as its placing will affect the cost of running service pipes to it. The route is to be determined by agreement under s 44(3) or by an arbitrator under s 44(4). Under the Water Act 1945, s 37 the duty was to lay a 'necessary main', and cases dealing with what is necessary under this section may still be relevant to the issue of the 'sufficiency' of supply. In *Cherwell District Council v Thames Water Authority* [1975] 1 WLR 448 the local authority wished to have a water supply to some proposed council houses. There was a piped supply nearby which could have served the houses. The local authority was willing to pay the cost of connecting the houses to this supply but the water authority requested in addition a contribution to the cost of a new 27 inch trunk main which was needed to serve the growing demands of the whole area. The local authority refused to pay the contribution. It was held that in the circumstances the trunk main was not a 'necessary main' for the proposed houses and that the local authority need not contribute. In the lower courts the question for consideration had been agreed by counsel to be whether a trunk main is in law capable of being a 'necessary main' [1973] 1 WLR 984 and [1974] 1 WLR 848 (CA). The House of Lords disapproved of this approach as it was not the question at issue in the case. The Lords held that the word 'necessary' is applicable only to a new main needed for no other purpose than to convey water from a starting point to a point at which it is practicable to connect to premises by a service pipe. In this case there was already a main to which the proposed houses could be connected. By contrast, in *Royco Homes v Southern Water Authority* [1979] 1 WLR 1366 (HL) developers had planning permission for the erection of 700 houses on a site and requisitioned the water authority to provide, under s 37(1) of the Water Act 1945, a domestic water supply to them. There was a 4-inch main in a nearby avenue but it was already fully committed and the authority proposed to lay an 8-inch main from a more distant 10-inch main. An 8-inch main was necessary to supply 700 houses. The developers were asked to deposit £115,000 as security for the annual sums falling due under the undertaking but they contended that their contribution should be limited to depositing as much money as would provide a main from the nearest main, the 4-inch one, and that the cost of bringing that main up to a suitable size to supply the site should be on the general body of ratepayers. It was held that: *(a)* the starting point for any main did not have to be the nearest existing main but the point where the new main could be fed with sufficient water, *(b)* what is a 'necessary main' is a question of fact and sound water engineering practice, *(c)* improvements to an existing distribution system at a point before the connection to the new development takes its departure cannot be charged against the developers. The developers were liable for the deposit claimed.

4 Constancy and pressure

By WIA, s 65(1) it shall be the duty of a water undertaker to cause the water in such of its mains or pipes as are used for providing supplies of water for domestic purposes or have fire-hydrants fixed on them to be laid on constantly and at such pressure as will cause the water to reach to the top of the top-most building in the undertaker's area. This does not include a duty to supply at a height greater than that to which the water will flow by gravitation through water mains from the service tank or reservoir from which the supply is taken or during any period when it is reasonable for the supply to be cut off or reduced for the purpose of carrying out any necessary works (s 65(2), (4)). The water undertaker can be liable on summary conviction to a fine for failure to carry out obligations under s 65 (s 65(10)) and the obligations are enforceable by the Secretary of State or the Director, under s 18.

5 Quality and sufficiency of water supplies

By WIA, s 68(1) it shall be the duty of the water undertaking, when supplying water for domestic or food production purposes, to supply only water which is wholesome at the time of supply; and so far as is reasonably practicable ensure that there is no deterioration in the quality of water. These duties are enforceable by the Secretary of State under s 18 (s 68(5)). By s 78, local authorities have a duty to notify a water authority of any unwhole-someness or insufficiency, actual or threatened, in the supply of water for domestic or food production purposes. Where piped water supplies in an area are insufficient or unwholesome, the local authority may require the water authority to provide a supply otherwise than in pipes, if this is practicable at reasonable cost (s 79). The local authority will be liable for the charges but can recover them from the owner or occupier of the premises to which the supply is made (s 79(4)).

By s 80, where premises are privately supplied with water for domestic or food production purposes, where the local authority is satisfied that the water is 'likely not to be wholesome' or may fail to be sufficient for domestic purposes, they may serve a notice specifying the steps required in their opinion for ensuring that the supply is wholesome and sufficient. By s 80(6) the steps to be taken may include requiring a supply to be taken from a water undertaker. By s 81 the recipients of a notice may appeal to the Secretary of State within the period specified (not less than 28 days from service) as the date on which it is to take effect. The duty is to supply 'wholesome' water. In *Read v Croydon Corporation* [1938] 4 All ER 631 (a case under a private Act where the duty was to supply 'pure and wholesome' water) it was held that there was a right of action by the daughter of a water rate payer when she contracted typhoid fever from contaminated water supplied by the corporation. In a Privy Council case, *AG v Lower Hutt Corporation* [1964] AC 1469, it was held that the adding of fluoride to the public water supply by a local authority in New Zealand was not a breach of an obligation to supply 'pure water'.

The Secretary of State has made regulations for preserving water quality, under s 69's predecessor, WA 1989, s 53; they are the Water Supply (Water Quality) Regulations 1989 (SI No 1147/1989) as amended by SI No 1383/1989, made pursuant to European Community Directive 80/778/EEC.

The water undertaker is guilty of an offence if water supplied by means of pipes to any premises is unfit for human consumption unless the undertakers prove that they had no reasonable grounds for suspecting that the water would be used for human consumption or that they exercised all due diligence for securing that the water was fit for human consumption on leaving their pipes (s 70(3)). This offence was introduced after the incident in Camelford, Cornwall, when 20 tonnes of aluminium sulphate was allowed to contaminate the drinking water supply. Unfitness is not defined; water which is unwholesome by the standards of the Water Quality Regulations made under s 67 is not necessarily unfit under s 70. An unpleasant smell or taste need not be a health risk.

6 Contamination, waste and misuse of water

By WIA, ss 71–75 various offences are constituted in relation to the misuse of water. If an owner or occupier of any premises to which a supply of water is made by the undertaker intentionally or negligently causes or suffers any water fitting for which he is responsible to be or remain so out of order or in need of repair that the water main is or is likely to be contaminated by the return to the pipe of any substance from the premises or the water supplied is likely to be contaminated before it is used or water is likely to be wasted or unduly consumed, he commits an offence (s 73(1)). If a person who is the owner or occupier of any premises supplies any of the water supplied to the premises to another person for use in other premises, or intentionally allows a person to take water for use in other premises unless for extinguishing a fire or to supply an unintentional lack of water there, he shall commit an offence, as shall the user of the improperly supplied water (s 73(2), (4)). Such an amount as is reasonable for the cost of the misused water can be recovered by the undertaker from the person liable (s 73(3)). Regulations may be made by the Secretary of State for preventing contamination, waste and misuse such as by forbidding the use of non-approved fittings or those made of non-approved materials (s 74(1)). A person designated in writing by a water undertaker or local authority may be empowered to enter any premises for the purpose of ascertaining whether any provision made with respect to any water fittings or the waste or misuse of water is being contravened (s 74(4)) and in order to prevent damage to persons or property may disconnect the service pipe in an emergency or serve notice on the consumer allowing him not less than seven days to carry out the work stated in the notice. In the case of emergency or the premises being unoccupied the undertaker may disconnect (s 75).

It is an offence to interfere intentionally or recklessly with any resource main, water main or other pipe vested in any water undertaker or by negligent act or omission to interfere with any main or other pipe or with any structure, installation or apparatus so as to damage it or have an effect on its use or operation; action taken in any emergency to prevent loss or damage to persons or property will be a defence (s 174(1), (2)).

Can a person be liable in negligence, nuisance or under the rule in *Rylands v Fletcher* (1866) LR 1 Ex 265 if pollution seeps from his premises and pollutes water which is to be abstracted for domestic purposes? In *Cambridge Water Co v Eastern Counties Leather PLC* [1994] 2 AC 264 (HL) solvent from a tannery seeped through the ground under the premises whence it was conveyed in percolating water to a borehole from which domestic water was abstracted, rendering the water unfit for human consumption. It was held that foreseeability of harm of the relevant type was a prerequisite of the recovery of damages in both nuisance and *Rylands v Fletcher*. Here it was not established that the pollution of the water supply was foreseeable and the owners of the tannery were not liable. There was also no liability in negligence.

7 Power to deal with foul water and pollution

Subject to Pt III of the WIA every water undertaker shall have power, on any land which belongs to the undertaker, or over which they have the necessary easement, to construct and maintain drains, sewers, watercourses, catchpits and other works to intercept, treat or dispose of any foul water arising or flowing upon that land or of otherwise preventing the pollution of any waters whether surface or underground from which an undertaker is entitled to take water (s 161).

8 Duties to make recreational facilities available

If a water undertaker is given permission to construct a reservoir in Wales which may permanently affect the area and is not primarily intended to benefit the inhabitants of that area, it shall be the duty of the undertaker to provide facilities for recreation or other leisure-time occupation for the benefit of those inhabitants (s 191(1)). A Code of Practice for recreation and sport on water undertakers' land has been promulgated under WIA, s 18.

9 Street works

By WIA, s 158(1) and WRA, s 159(1) relevant undertakers (water or sewer authorities) have power, for the purpose of carrying out their functions, to lay a 'relevant pipe' in, under or over a street, keep it there, inspect, repair or alter it and carry out incidental works for breaking open or tunnelling under the street or breaking up or opening any sewer, drain or tunnel. 'Relevant pipe' is a water main, resource main, discharge or service pipe (for water) and a sewer or disposal main (in relation to a sewerage undertaker) (WIA, s 158(7), WRA, s 160(4)). Water (and sewerage) authorities are subject to the provisions of the New Roads and Street Works Act 1991, Pt III and under that Act must give due notice to bodies involved of their intention to carry out work (such as to gas, electricity and fire authorities), take any special precautions required by the nature of the work (such as whether they will cause traffic diversions) and make due reinstatement of the road.

Compensation is payable for damage done in the course of carrying out the works (WIA, s 180 and Sched 12, para 2; WRA, s 177 and Sched 21). It shall be the duty of the water undertaker to keep records of every resource main, water main or discharge pipe vested in them and of any underground works vested in them and make them available free of charge to the public for inspection at reasonable times (WIA, s 198(1)).

10 Works on private land

By WRA, s 160(1) and WIA, s 159 the authority may lay a relevant pipe in any land, inspect, repair or alter any such pipe and carry out 'any works incidental' to those purposes. In *Hutton v Esher UDC* [1974] Ch 167 (CA) it was held that the phrase was wide enough to permit the demolition of a private house if the execution of the works required it.

11 Water resources

By WRA, s 19 it shall be the duty of the National Rivers Authority to take such action as it may from time to time consider necessary or expedient for conserving, redistributing or otherwise augmenting water resources in England and Wales and of securing the proper use of water resources. It shall make water resources management schemes with water undertakers and prescribe minimum acceptable river flows (ss 20, 21). It shall grant water abstraction licences (ss 34, 38, 39, 40, 46). The Secretary of State may make general drought orders authorising measures to deal with a shortage of water in an area (WRA, ss 73–81).

12 Planning consultation

By the Town and Country Planning General Development Order 1988 (SI No 1813), art 18, before granting planning permission for development on certain matters the local planning authority is required to consult the National Rivers Authority. Those matters include: development involving mining operations; that involving carrying out works in the bed or on the bank of a river or stream; using land for storing mineral oils and their derivatives; using land for the deposit of refuse or waste; the retention, treatment or disposal of sewage, trade-waste, slurry or sludge (except in the laying of sewers, making pumphouses in a line of sewers, tanks and cess-pits serving single houses or caravans); and the use of land as a cemetery.

13 Compulsory acquisition

A water or sewerage undertaker may be authorised by the Secretary of State to purchase compulsorily any land anywhere in England or Wales which is required by the undertaker for its purposes in carrying out its functions (WIA, s 155). The power includes creating and then acquiring new rights and also extinguishing rights (s 155(2)). By s 158 pipes and sewers laid by an undertaker under the provisions of Pt IV shall vest in the body which laid them. By s 183 nothing in the Act which empowers a body to carry on works shall entitle them to affect injuriously (unless with consent) works or property of certain undertakings listed in Sched 13, being, for example, undertakings of the National Rivers Authority, the Civil Aviation Authority, the British Coal Corporation, an undertaking running a telecommunications system, a public gas supplier, a licensed electricity generator or supplier, a public utility undertaking or British Railways. The procedure for compulsory acquisition is found in Sched 11 and in the Acquisition of Land Act 1981 and the Compulsory Purchase Act 1965. Compensation is made on the basis of the market value of the landowner's interest, excluding any additional value attributable to the proposed scheme.

14 Compensation

Compensation is payable for damage done to the land or for injurious affection of it (WIA, s 155 and Sched 11). Examples are manholes or inspection chambers in the land permanently interfering with cultivation, and disturbance to existing crops whilst the main is being laid; it is relevant to consider whether, because of the existence of the main, a possible alternative use of the land such as for house building is totally or partially prevented.

By WIA, s 180 and Sched 12 a relevant authority shall pay compensation to anyone who has sustained damage by reason of the exercise of its powers. In *Leonidis v Thames Water Authority* (1979) 77 LGR 722 a water authority, whilst repairing a sewer, blocked the normal entrance to the plaintiff's garage for eleven months and he suffered loss of profit. It was held that he could recover the loss of £2,500. The fact that the authority did not take an unreasonably long time on the job did not relieve them from liability; the plaintiff must not suffer virtual confiscation of his rights. The damage was not too remote. The land had suffered loss during the period because during that time its letting value must have been diminished.

In relation to compensation for pipe laying, matters to be considered include payments for a water main easement the payment for which is in practice assessed on so much a metre of run, based on 50 per cent of the vacant possession value of a notional easement strip. In a helpful booklet, *Wayleaves and Easements*, published by the Country Landowners Association (W3/1989) it is suggested that the minimum width needed to protect the pipe is 10 feet on either side, plus the diameter of the pipe. In addition to payment for an easement there should be a claim for compensation for manholes, valves and other structures whether or not above ground. Under a national agreement made in 1989 British Telecom pay an annual wayleave of £12.66 for an above ground manhole, for loss to agricultural operations. The laying of the pipe will cause damage, disturbance and loss of profits and the professional fees for negotiating all the matters may also be claimed. It is advised by the CLA that when the landowner receives notice of an intended scheme the following should be discussed: record of condition (for reinstatement purposes); means of access for the undertakers to do the work; reinstatement of land drainage severed by the pipe-line; protection of ditches under which the pipe-line is to run; depth of pipe, at least 900mm below the original surface is suggested; replacement of top soil after laying. The British Standards Association publication, *Pipelines on Land: General* BS 8010 should be consulted.

The fact that the authority can enter in future to inspect and repair will affect the value of the land, and the compensation payment will take account of this (*Markland v Cannock Rural District Council* (1973) 227 EG 1173). In *Griffiths v Swansea Corporation; Morris's Trustees v Swansea Corporation* (1960) 11 P & CR 470, the local authority laid a trunk main 3,657 yards long, with one manhole and three valve chambers, in the land of the claimants. The first claimant was awarded £145 in respect of the pipe 1,123 yards long and £17 for the valve chambers, and the second £175 for the pipe 2,534 yards long and £16 for the chambers. Both were awarded costs. Any immediate enhancement of value to the land must be set off against the claim. For example, the laying of the main may make the land more readily saleable for housing development if the owner or occupier would have a right to connect to the main.

It was held in *St John's College, Oxford v Thames Water Authority* [1990] 1 EGLR 229 that an underground water main laid with an average working width of excavation of 22 feet sterilised the whole strip of land through which it passed so far as any future building over it was concerned and that there was damage or injurious affection to the whole land so far as the reversions on the tenancies on the farms were concerned. The test of damage was loss of value to the owners. The Lands Tribunal held that it was inappropriate to award 'recognition payments' or 'right of entry payments' as had customarily been done in the past.

In *Rickmansworth Water Co v J W Ward & Son Ltd* [1990] EGCS 91 the plaintiffs obtained a mandatory injunction (suspended for one year) that the defendants should remove a timber-drying building erected innocently and with planning permission by them over the plaintiffs' water main and six metre wide inspection strip. There was no duty on the plaintiffs to advise the defendants prior to building that no construction could take place; the defendants had paid compensation to the then landowner on acquiring their easement, under the Water Act 1945, s 19 and Sched 3.

There can be a set-off of compensation for enhancement. In *Collins v Thames Water Utilities Ltd* (1994) 9449 EG 116 (Lands Tribunal) a sewer was laid under WIA, Sched 12, across the foot of the garden of a private house at a depth of 700mm, with a protected area of 6m, amounting to 36 per cent of the garden. The house was then connected to the new sewer with 419 other houses, and the septic tank which had served it was not needed. Compensation of £415 was awarded for entry, disturbance and claimants' time. Nothing was payable for alleged injurious affection, any detriment in future was negligible and the enhancement of the property's drainage must be set off against it.

If the works of the authority cause loss of profit to the owner or occupier of land but are wholly carried out on the land of someone else, it does not appear that the owner or occupier can recover his lost profit from the authority, if the acquisition is made under s 68 of the Lands Clauses Consolidation Act 1845 (as continued by the Compulsory Purchase Act 1965, s 10), or any Act which incorporates its terms (*Argyle Motors Ltd v Birkenhead Corporation* [1975] AC 99 (HL)). But if the claim is made under some other Act, such as the Gas Act 1986, s 9(3) and Sched 4, it is possible that compensation may be awarded for loss of profit, if *Leonidis's* case is followed. See the discussion in (1974) *Journal of Planning Law*, 257, at 263 (Jones and Wilkinson).

Chapter 7

Sewers and Drains

The Water Act 1989 transferred to sewerage undertakers the functions of water authorities relating to the provision of sewerage services and Sched 8 of the Act made amendments to the enactments relating to the transferred functions.

The Water Industry Act 1991, the Water Resources Act 1991, the Statutory Water Companies Act 1991, the Water Consolidation (Consequential Provisions) Act 1991 and the Environmental Protection Act 1990 codify the law relating to water and sewage and add new provisions for the protection of the environment. Sewerage services are dealt with in the Water Industry Act 1991 ('WIA'), Pt IV.

By WIA, s 94(1) it shall be the duty of every sewerage undertaker:

(a) to provide, improve and extend such a system of public sewers (whether inside its area or elsewhere) and so to cleanse and maintain those sewers as to ensure that that area is and continues to be effectually drained; and

(b) to make provision for the emptying of those sewers and such further provision (whether inside its area or elsewhere) as is necessary from time to time for effectually dealing, by means of sewage disposal works or otherwise, with the contents of those sewers.

It was held in *Tayside Regional Council v Secretary of State for Scotland* (1995) *The Times*, 28 January that where a private party proposed to connect a drain or private sewer to a public sewer, the fact that the public sewer was already overloaded was not necessarily a valid ground upon which the sewerage authority could refuse permission for the connection. The case turned on the interpretation and relationship of ss 1 and 12(5) of the Sewerage

(Scotland) Act 1968 (the general equivalent of WIA, ss 94(1) and 98(1)).

The duties of the undertaker shall be enforceable by the Secretary of State under s 18 or by the Director General of Water Services. The Secretary may make regulations which will facilitate the determination of the extent to which an undertaker is failing in its duties and the regulations can include provisions for payment of money by an undertaker to a person who is affected by a failure to reach performance standards (WIA, s 95(3)).

1 Construction of sewers and drains

The Water Industry Act 1991, s 219(1) states that 'sewer' includes all sewers and drains (not being drains as mentioned below) which are used for the drainage of buildings and yards appurtenant to buildings. By s 219(2), references to a pipe, including references to a main, a drain or a sewer, shall include references to a tunnel or conduit which serves or is to serve as the pipe in question and references to sewage disposal works shall include references to the machinery and equipment of those works. By s 219(2) 'drain' means (subject to subs (2)) a drain used for the drainage of one building or of any buildings or yards appurtenant to buildings within the same curtilage (a sewer normally drains more than one building). However, in *J Pullan & Sons v Leeds City Council* [1990] EGCS 101 (CA) a developer made an agreement with the council that if he constructed a sewer for a large area of development land, the council would declare it to be vested in them. The 'sewer' was made but only one property, a factory for Rank Hovis McDougal, was connected. The authority refused to adopt but it was held that this was a sewer, even though connected to one building; the test was not whether the article was performing functions but whether it could be described as an article for performing them. In *Blackdown Properties v Ministry of Housing and Local Government* [1967] Ch 115 a sewer was constructed for use on an estate but part was no longer needed so it was sealed off. It was held that it was still a sewer. Once it was established that the sewer was a pipe to drain buildings, it remained a sewer despite non-use. 'Used for drainage' in s 343 of the Public Health Act 1936 did not require current use but connoted the pipe's function.

A sewer does not necessarily carry sewage; it could also carry flood or rain water, for example (*Hutton v Esher Urban District*

Council [1974] Ch 167 (CA)). A sewer not draining buildings (such as a cesspit at a caravan site) is not within the definition, apparently. In *Dear v Thames Water* (1994) 33 Con LR 43 it was held that a culverted watercourse in private land was neither a sewer nor a drain and the local authority (which had day-to-day responsibility for maintenance under the Water Act 1973, s 15) was not liable when it overflowed because of throttling up after a storm; the authority's 'beneficent acts' of maintenance over the culvert did not impose liability on it, as the riparian owners were responsible for its upkeep and control of it had not been taken from them by the authority.

In *British Railways Board v Tonbridge and Malling District Council* (1981) 79 LGR 565 (CA) three natural watercourses had been culverted under a railway line. Over the years the surface water from a considerable number of streets and houses had been piped into the watercourses. It was held that the culvert was not a sewer within the Public Health Act 1936, s 343 (the relevant provision). The fact that surface drainage from a built-up area had been channelled into the watercourses was insufficient to make the culvert a drain 'used for the drainage of buildings'.

It is a question of fact whether a structure is one building or more than one. In *Hedley v Webb* [1901] 2 Ch 126 a pair of semis was held to be one building; in *Humphery v Young* [1903] 1 KB 44 each semi-detached house was held to be a separate building. In *Weaver v Family Housing Association (York) Ltd* (1975) 74 LGR 255 (HL) pipes from each of a group of terraced houses ran into a common 6-inch pipe under one of them. The common pipe was held to be a sewer. In *Cook v Minion* (1978) 37 P & CR 58 a pipe connected four or five houses, then it ran into a 4-inch pipe which joined the local authority sewer. It was held that the 4-inch pipe was not a sewer.

A drain and a private sewer are the responsibility of the individual; a public sewer is the responsibility of the sewerage undertaker. 'Public sewer' is defined in WIA 1991, s 219(1). The authority acquires an absolute property in the sewer and the space which it occupies; its interest is an estate in fee simple which will determine if the sewer ceases to be a sewer, and this is a fee simple absolute by virtue of the Law of Property Act 1925, s 7(1) (*Tithe Redemption Commission v Runcorn Urban District Council* [1954] Ch 383 (CA)). The rights of any person entitled to use the sewer before a declaration of adoption are preserved (WIA, s 102(6)); this includes a prescriptive right (*AG v Dorking Union*

Guardians (1882) 20 ChD 595). If the sewerage authority does not own the land through which the sewer runs, it acquires a right of subjacent support by implication and the landowner is entitled to compensation (*Re Dudley Corporation* (1881–2) 8 QBD 86). The authority probably also has a right of support from adjacent land, at least so far as the adjacent land is in the same ownership as that occupied by the sewer (*Jary v Barnsley Corporation* [1907] 2 Ch 600, at 613).

By WIA, s 94(1) the sewerage authority is under a duty to provide a system of public sewers and 'so to cleanse and maintain them as to ensure that the area is and continues to be effectually drained'. It must also make provision for the emptying of the sewers and such further provision as is necessary for effectually dealing with the contents, by sewage disposal works or otherwise, *ibid*.

Although the authority must decide when sewers are necessary it may not defer the decision unreasonably (in *R v Secretary of State, ex p Jaywick Sands Freeholders Association Ltd* [1975] JPL 663, sewers and water supply were not provided for 773 holiday chalets after twenty years; delay unreasonable, mandamus issued).

A breach of WIA, s 94 by the authority does not give rise to an action by an individual; the duty is not owed to a specific person or group of persons. In *Weaver v Yorkshire Water Authority* [1981] CLY 2874 a public sewer passed beneath the plaintiff's house and on occasion became blocked at an interceptor trap, because foreign bodies were put into the sewer by third parties. This flooded the plaintiff's cellar. The sewer was adequate for the plaintiff's house and the other houses which it served. The water authority offered to remove the trap and seal off this exit but the plaintiff refused and claimed an injunction for the authority to divert the sewer. Held: (*a*) on the facts there was no breach of the Water Act 1973, s 14 (now WIA, s 94); (*b*) no duty was owed under s 14 to the plaintiff or to any person or group of persons. The sewerage authority may arrange for the local authority to exercise the sewerage functions of the authority on an agency basis (WIA, s 97).

If the authority fails to provide a sufficient sewer it is not permitted to solve its problem by calling upon householders to stop using the sewer, even if the householders originally made a connection into the sewer without permission from the authority (*Fordom v Parsons* [1894] 2 QB 780, a case under the similar s 15 of the Public Health Act 1875). But an individual who is caused damage by the authority's failure to provide an adequate sewer can make no claim against the authority (*Clark v Epsom Rural District Council* [1929] 1 Ch 287). In *Robinson v Workington Corporation* [1897] 1 QB 619 an overloaded sewer flooded Robinson's houses. He failed in his claim for damages. It was held that his remedy was to complain to the Local Government Board under the Public Health Act 1875: the remedy now is a complaint to the Secretary of State or the Director General of Water Services, who may make an enforcement order against the authority under WIA, s 18 compelling the authority to discharge its functions in such manner and at such time as the order directs. Lord Esher said in *Robinson's* case, at 621, that if a duty is imposed by statute and the duty would not exist apart from the statute, and a remedy for default or breach is provided by the statute which creates the duty, there is no other remedy available to an aggrieved person. On the other hand, if the authority tries to remedy a defect or inadequacy of the sewer and does it so negligently as to create a nuisance, an action by the individual who suffers damage will lie, *Smeaton v Ilford Corporation* [1954] Ch 450. The principles of law concerning the exercise by authorities of their statutory duties were analysed in *Department of Transport v North West Water Authority* [1983] 3 WLR 707. A nuisance brought about by the gradual operation of the elements is not actionable. In *Radstock Co-operative Society Ltd v Norton Radstock Urban District Council* [1968] Ch 605, the urban district council laid a sewer under a river bed. After a time the river washed away the bed and exposed the sewer. The sewer caused eddies in the river and these damaged the plaintiff's land. The council was held not liable in nuisance. Some damage is too remote. In *Lamb v Camden London Borough Council* [1981] 2 WLR 1038 (CA) it was held that it is not reasonably foreseeable that if in repairing a sewer an authority breaks a water pipe, causing a nearby house to be damaged and so left unoccupied, squatters will move into it and cause damage to the house. In such a case the authority is not liable in nuisance or negligence for the damage. In *Leonidis v Thames Water Authority* (1979) 77 LGR 722 it was held that loss of profit to a garage, caused when the nearby access road was obstructed for 11 months by repairs to a sewer, was recoverable from the water authority even though the work was done under statutory authority and did not take an unreasonably long time, the garage not being totally closed.

Although the authority is under a duty to provide such sewers as may be necessary to drain its area effectually it cannot be required to provide a sewer for every house wherever situated (*Kinson Pottery Co Ltd v Poole Corporation* [1899] 2 QB 41, at 49: house half a mile from existing sewer) unless the owner or occupier will give the sewerage authority financial guarantees under WIA, s 99. A planning application can be refused for inadequate sewerage arrangements despite the right under s 98 for the owner to demand a sewer, *Wimpey & Co Ltd v Secretary of State and Maidstone DC* [1978] JPL 773.

A sewerage authority must make available for public inspection records showing all public sewers in its area and distinguishing those which are for surface water from those which are for foul water (WIA, ss 199, 200). The fact that a sewer is shown on such a map is not conclusive evidence that it has been duly adopted by the local authority by resolution under WIA, s 102. It may have been acquired by the authority by some other method, such as by passing with the soil of a highway under the maxim *quicquid plantatur solo, solo cedit* (*Royco Homes Ltd v Eatonwill Construction Ltd* [1979] Ch 276). Where an authority (not being a collection authority) provides pipes for collecting or disposing of waste or of anything produced from waste, or heat, air, steam or water produced from waste, or outfall pipes for sewage disposal, it must send a map showing the location of the pipes to the collection authority (Control of Pollution Act 1974, s 28). In England and Wales the collection authority is the district council or London borough (1974 Act, s 30).

Plans for a building or extension which are submitted for approval under the Building Regulations 1991 (SI No 2768) may be rejected or conditionally approved by the local authority if the building work is to be carried out over a sewer, drain or pipe (Building Act 1984, s 18). For example, conditions may be imposed that the sewer is to be protected against settlement caused by the weight of the building.

By the Town and Country Planning Act 1990, s 65, and the Town and Country Planning General Development Order 1988 (SI No 1813) art 11(1)(*d*) and Sched 4, Pt 2, development consisting of the construction of buildings or other operations or the use of land for retaining, treating or disposing of sewage, trade waste or sludge (other than the laying of sewers, pumphouses in a line of sewers, septic tanks and cesspools serving single houses, single buildings or single caravans in which not more than ten persons normally reside or congregate) must be advertised in a local newspaper at least 21 days before being determined by the planning authority. In addition a notice in the prescribed form must be prominently displayed on the land for not less than seven days in the month immediately preceding the application. By Sched 2, Pt 16 of the 1988 Order any development not above ground on behalf of a sewerage authority required in connection with the provision, improvement, maintenance or repair of a sewer, outfall pipe, sludge main or associated apparatus, has planning permission without the need of an express application. By Pt 10 of the Order, works of inspection, repair or renewal of any sewer, main, pipe or other apparatus, including breaking open any land for that purpose, are also permitted without application for permission.

2 Requisitioning of sewers

It shall be the duty of a sewerage undertaker to provide a public sewer to be used for the drainage for domestic purposes of premises in a locality if a person entitled to do so requires it by notice (WIA, s 94(1)). The persons so entitled are the owner or occupier of premises, the local authority, a Commission for New Towns, the Development Board for Rural Wales or an urban development corporation (s 98(2)). The drainage of domestic premises means such domestic sewerage purposes as are specified in a requirement for the premises (s 98(4)). The undertaker shall not be in default unless it has not laid a public sewer within six months of the 'relevant day' (s 101(1)), but that day is not until any reasonable financial stipulations imposed by the undertaker as a condition of laying the sewer have been agreed to by the requisitioner (s 98).

In *William Leech (Midlands) Ltd v Severn Trent Water Authority* (1981) 260 EG 1123 (CA) a developer of a site of 61 houses brought the private sewer to point *A*. The water authority on receiving a requisition from him proposed to bring the public sewer to point *B* which was a higher level and in a different part of the site. A pump and rising main would have been needed to make the communication. It was held that the authority must provide a communicating sewer and not merely a sewer which the developer can cause to communicate, though the manner and place of communication were by s 16(3)(*a*) of the Water Act 1973 (now WIA, s 101(3)) placed within the discretion of the water authority. It was held in *Tayside Regional Council v Secretary of*

State for Scotland (1995) *The Times,* 28 January that where a private party proposed to connect a drain or private sewer to a public sewer, the fact that the public sewer was already overloaded was not necessarily a valid ground for refusal of permission for the connection. The case interpreted ss 1 and 12(5) of the Sewerage (Scotland) Act 1968 (general equivalent of WIA 1991, ss 94(1) and 98(1)).

The owner or occupier who requisitions a public sewer must give certain financial guarantees to help towards its cost, on a formula given in s 99. In such a case the authority may require security for 12 annual payments, to be made following the provision of the sewer. They are calculated at such a sum as does not exceed the 'relevant deficit' (defined in s 100) on the sewer in each year. If the undertaker is liable to provide a sewer under s 98 and fails avoidably to do so within six months or such longer period as the parties may agree, the authority is liable in damages (s 98(4)).

This power to requisition the provision of public sewers may help to avoid the situation where planning permission is refused on the ground that adequate sewers are not available to the proposed development.

A person is not liable for a full sewerage charge if his premises are not connected to a sewer (*Daymond v Plymouth City Council* [1976] AC 609) but can be liable to pay a reduced rate for such services as are provided by the authority (WIA, s 142). In *South West Water Authority v Rumble's* [1985] 1 All ER 513 (HL) it was held that a person who had no water supply or drainage was nonetheless liable for a rate as the roof on premises over his shop drained into the sewer.

An owner or occupier of premises is entitled to have his drain or sewer connected to the public sewer. Before connecting he must give notice of his wishes to the sewerage authority and the authority can refuse if the construction or condition of the drain is such that its connection would be prejudicial to the general system (s 106(4)). In Greater London the authority may refuse 'on such grounds as it thinks fit' (s 106(8)). If the authority consents, it may superintend the connecting up (s 108(1)) or it may insist on doing the work at the applicant's expense (s 107(1)). He may be required to lodge security for the expense (s 107(3)). No one may empty into the public sewer any matter which is likely to injure the sewer, interfere with its flow or prejudicially affect the treatment of its contents, or any chemicals or heated liquid if these things would be likely to be prejudicial to health, or any petroleum spirit or calcium carbide (s 106(2)).

3 Sewer agreements

By WIA, s 104 a sewerage authority may agree with any person who is constructing or proposing to construct a sewer that if the sewer is constructed in accordance with the terms of the agreement they will declare the sewer or works to be vested in them and the agreement will then become enforceable against the authority by the owner or occupier of any premises served by the sewer or works. In *Royco Homes Ltd v Eatonwill Construction Ltd* [1979] Ch 276, a local authority failed to pass a formal resolution under the Public Health Act 1936, s 17 to adopt a sewer made by a developer but adopted as a public highway the lane through which it ran. It was held that the correspondence about adoption between the developer and the authority did not constitute an adoption agreement under s 18 (now WIA, s 102(1)) but that the authority had 'acquired' the sewer by virtue of the legal maxim that whatever is contained in the soil is part of the soil unless there is something to displace the effect of the maxim (see the statement of the principle in *Simmons v Midford* [1969] Ch 415 at 420). No drain (as defined in WIA, s 219(1)) can be a public sewer. It was held in *Hutton v Esher UDC* [1973] 2 WLR 917 (CA) that a pipe which had three functions, including that of a surface water sewer, could be a public sewer. It is common for authorities to impose their own criteria on the provision of pipes and pumping stations and to demand commuted sum payments for adoption under s 102 agreements. It is suggested that their discretion is wide but that they cannot demand more than sound sewer engineering practice would dictate, by analogy with *Royco Homes v Southern Water Authority* [1979] 1 WLR 1366 (HL).

4 Drainage of existing buildings

The local authority has powers concerning the drainage of existing buildings: where satisfactory provision has not been made for drainage and ought to be made, or any cesspool, private sewer or drain is insufficient or admits subsoil water or is in a condition making it prejudicial to health or a nuisance by reason of being no longer used, or for any other reason, then the local authority can give notice requiring the owner or occupier to carry out the necessary works to remedy these defects (Building Act 1984, s 59(1)). If premises, though adequately drained, are served by a system which is not adapted to the general sewerage scheme of the neighbourhood or is otherwise objectionable, the water authority may, at the authority's expenses, insist on the premises being connected to and using the general sewerage scheme in place of the former system (WIA, s 113(1)). If the drainage is ineffectual the local authority can use the provisions of s 114 and require necessary works to be done at the owner's or occupier's expense.

A pipe used to convey rainwater from a roof may not be used also as a soil pipe from a sanitary convenience and a pipe for surface water may not act as a ventilating shaft for a foul water pipe (Building Act 1984, s 60(1)). The soil pipe from a water-closet must be properly ventilated (s 60(2)). If the contents of a cesspool overflow or leak away the local authority may by notice require the owner or occupier to carry out such works as are necessary to prevent this from recurring (Public Health Act 1936, s 50).

A person in a local authority area may not alter the course of any underground drain which communicates with a sewer or cesspool, except in an emergency, without giving at least 24 hours notice to the local authority of his intention to do so; the local authority must be given free access to the work (Building Act 1984, s 61).

Where it appears to a sewerage undertaker that there are reasonable grounds for believing that a drain or private sewer connecting with a public sewer is in such a condition as to be injurious or likely to cause injury to health or be a nuisance; or any such drain or sewer is so defective as to admit subsoil water, the undertaker may examine it. If it is found to be in proper condition the undertaker must reinstate it and make good any damage caused (WIA, s 114).

5 New buildings

The local authority (the district council or London borough council, Building Act 1984, s 126) may not approve plans for a new building unless it is satisfied that satisfactory provision is made for drainage or that such provision may be dispensed with (s 21). Unless a proposed drain connects with a sewer or cesspool, it cannot be considered satisfactory (s 21(4)). But if the plans show that the drainage for the building will be satisfactory, consent to the application cannot be refused on the ground that the sewer to which the drain will connect is unsatisfactory (*Chesterton Rural District Council v Ralph Thompson Ltd* [1947] KB 300). If there is not a sewer within 100 feet of the building, connection to it cannot be insisted upon unless the local authority agrees to bear the cost of making that part of the connection which is beyond 100 feet (s 21(4), (5)). A formal resolution of the authority is necessary to make the authority liable; the agreement of their surveyor alone was held not binding on the local authority in *Princes Investments Ltd v Frimley and Camberley Urban District Council* [1962] 1 QB 681. In *Myrick v Pembroke Corporation* (1912) 76 JP 365, a house was over 119 feet from the available sewer but there was a privy at the boundary wall of the house less than 30 feet from the sewer and an out-building less than 99 feet from the sewer. When the owner failed to comply with a notice to connect, the local authority coverted the privy into a water closet and successfully claimed the cost from the owner as it was held that the building was within 100 feet of the sewer because its outbuildings were within this distance. Connection with the sewer cannot be insisted on if the sewer is not at a level which makes it reasonably practicable to connect to it, or the intervening land is not land through which the owner is entitled to put his drain, or the sewer is not a public one or one that he is entitled to use (s 21(4)). The local authority must be satisfied that there is satisfactory provision for the drainage of both waste water and rainwater from the proposed new building (s 21(2)). See also Building Regulations 1991 (SI 2768, in force from 1 June 1992 (discussed later)).

6 Street works

The sewerage or water authority has power to break open streets in order to lay such things as sewers and water pipes (WIA, s 158(1)). Where the highway authority (which may be the local authority) proposes to carry out works which will disturb the equipment of a statutory undertaker, such as a public gas supplier or Area Electricity Board, the authority must give notice to the undertaker specifying the works and the undertaker may serve notice in turn listing what it requires to be done to protect the apparatus from damage, at the authority's expense. A dispute will go to arbitration. Where it is the statutory undertaker which proposes to break up the street, ss 54–56 of the New Roads and

Street Works Act 1991 lay down a procedure for giving notice to the highway authority or, in the case of a private street, to those having the management or control of the street. By s 59 of the same Act a street authority shall use their best endeavours to co-ordinate the execution of works of all kinds in the interests of safety and so as to minimise the inconvenience to persons using the street.

Where a statutory undertaker causes a nuisance which is attributable to its carrying out of street works under its statutory powers, the authority is not liable unless it has also been negligent (*Department of Transport v North West Water Authority* [1983] 3 WLR 707 (HL), construing s 18(2) of the Public Utilities Street Works Act 1950). 'Negligence' in this context means failing to carry out the work and to conduct the operation with all reasonable regard and care for the interests of other persons, *Allen v Gulf Oil Refining Ltd* [1981] AC 1001, Lord Wilberforce at 1011.

7 Building Regulations 1991

Local authority building byelaws have been superseded by building regulations made under the Building Act 1984, s 1. The current regulations are the Building Regulations 1991 (SI No 2768). The Building Regulations apply to the construction of new buildings in England or Wales and the alteration or extension of existing buildings (reg 3(1)). Notification to the local authorities in whose area the work will be carried out is necessary.

By s 6 of the Building Act 1984 the Secretary of State is empowered to issue practical guidance documents which supply the detail which was formerly in the Regulations. He has issued Approved Documents in conjunction with them, on such subjects as structure, ventilation, drainage and waste disposal (*Encyclopaedia of Environmental Health* (Sweet & Maxwell) vol 4, page 5384/3 *et seq*).

A person who has building work done may at his option choose to have it inspected by an 'approved inspector' and in such a case the local authority's functions of inspection will not be exerciseable, ss 47–53. By s 54 approved public bodies may be their own inspectors, on terms (Sched 4). Both provisions are covered by the Building (Approved Inspectors) Regulations 1985 (SI No 1066).

By reg 11 of the Building Regulations 1991 a person who intends to carry out building work or to make a material change of use shall give to the local authority a 'building notice' in accord with reg 12 or deposit plans with the authority under reg 13. Consultation with the fire authority may also be necessary, reg 11(2).

Before building work is commenced and at specified stages of the work, notice must be given to the authority at least 48 hours before commencing work and at least 24 hours before covering any drain or private sewer, reg 14. The local authority may test any such drain or private sewer to establish whether it complies with Pt H of Sched 1, reg 15.

By Sched 1:

(i) *Site preparation* Precautions shall be taken to avoid danger to health from substances on or in the ground, C2. Subsoil drainage shall be provided to avoid ground moisture passing into the building, C3.

(ii) *Means of ventilation* An adequate supply of air shall be provided for persons in the building, F1.

(iii) *Hygiene* A bathroom containing a fixed bath or shower bath shall be provided for all dwellings, G4. Sufficient sanitary conveniences shall be provided, G4.

(iv) *Sanitary pipework and drainage* Any system carrying foul water from the premises to the foul water outfall shall be adequate, H1. Cesspools, septic tanks and settlement tanks shall be constructed to permit access for emptying and to avoid contamination by their contents, H2. The rainwater drainage system shall be adequate, H3.

(v) *Heat producing appliances* Fixed heat producing appliances must have an adequate supply of air for efficient combustion and adequate means of discharge of the products of combustion. They must be so placed as to reduce the risk of causing fire, J1 to 3.

(vi) *Insulation of heating services* Heat water pipes and warm air ducts shall have adequate thermal insulation unless they are intended to contribute to the heating of the building, L5.

The Approved Documents, which replace the Building Regulations Manual, give detailed guidance and illustrations on all the above matters.

8 Statutory nuisances

By the Environmental Protection Act 1990 (EPA), s 80(1) where a local authority is satisfied that a statutory nuisance exists or is likely to recur in its area, it shall serve on the person responsible notice requiring its abatement and/or prohibiting its recurrence and/or requiring the execution of certain works or the taking of steps, as may be necessary for those purposes. If an abatement notice is, without reasonable excuse, not complied with, the recipient commits an offence for which there can be imposed a fine not exceeding level 5, and daily penalties (s 80(4), (5)). It is a defence to show that the best practicable means were used to prevent or counteract the effects of the nuisance (s 80(7)). A 'person aggrieved' by a nuisance may complain to a magistrates court which can then make an abatement order (and a recurrence order to prevent repetition) and impose a fine (s 82(1)).

It is the duty of a local authority to cause its area to be inspected from time to time to detect any statutory nuisance on premises and to serve a notice on the person causing or permitting a nuisance, or, if he cannot be found, then on the owner or occupier of the premises, requiring him to abate it and to carry out such work as shall be necessary for that purpose (EPA, s 79). If the occupier has not caused the nuisance and the person responsible cannot be found the local authority may abate the nuisance and charge the cost to the person liable (EPA, s 81(4)). Examples of statutory nuisances are any pond, pool, ditch, gutter or watercourse which is so foul or in such a state as to be prejudicial to health or a nuisance (s 259; a sewer is not included in this phrase: *R v Parlby* (1889) 22 QBD 520), and any well, tank, cistern or water-butt used for the supply of water for domestic purposes which is so placed, constructed or kept as to render the water liable to be contaminated to an extent prejudicial to health (s 141). There is also power to close a polluted well, tank or other source of supply (s 140).

9 Waste

By EPA, s 33(1) a person shall not deposit controlled waste, or knowingly permit it to be deposited in or on any land or dispose of it in a manner likely to cause pollution of the environment or harm to human health, without a current waste management licence. By s 75(4) 'controlled waste' means 'household, industrial and commercial waste or any such waste'. The licences are issued by the waste regulation authority, which is the county council for a non-metropolitan county in England and Wales, the London Waste Authority for Greater London, the district council in a non-metropolitan county, the Greater Manchester WDA or the Merseyside WDA; in Wales it is the district council and in Scotland the islands or district council (EPA, s 30(1)). By s 3(3) of the

Environment Act 1995, waste regulation authorities are required to make a scheme of transfer of appropriate property to the Environment Agency established by s 1(1) of the 1995 Act and many of their functions will then be exercised by the Agency (s 2(1)). This chapter should be read accordingly.

The Secretary of State has issued a Code of Practice under EPA, s 34(7) on *Waste Management: the duty of care.* It affects anyone who produces, imports, carries, keeps or disposes of controlled waste. By s 34(10) a code is admissible in evidence and may be taken into account in proceedings under the Act.

By EPA, s 45(1) it shall be the duty of each waste collection authority to arrange for the collection of household waste in its area (unless the cost would be unreasonably high). By s 49(1) the authority must consider the feasibility of recycling waste.

The Waste Management Licensing Framework Directive on Waste (Circular 11/94) gives guidance on the Waste Management Regulations 1994 (SI No 1056/1994).

The discharge of trade effluent into sewers may be permitted in certain circumstances, under WIA, ss 106 and 108. No one may commence to drain trade effluent into a sewer without giving notice to the disposal authority of the type and volume of the proposed discharge and obtaining the authority's consent (WIA, s 118). Trade effluent is liquid, with or without particles in suspension, which is produced in the course of any trade or industry carried on at trade premises, excluding domestic sewage (WIA, s 141(1)). In *Yorkshire Dyeing and Proofing Co Ltd v Middleton Borough Council* [1953] 1 WLR 393 it was held that where trade effluent was lawfully discharged from one set of premises and fresh premises were obtained in addition, the effluent from the new premises could not lawfully be sent into the sewer through the old premises without fresh notice and permission from the authority even though no greater quantity or different type of trade effluent was being passed into the sewer. It was held in *Thames Water Authority v Blue and White Launderettes Ltd* [1980] 1 WLR 700 (CA) that the discharge from launderette washing machines was trade effluent although it was the same as a discharge from domestic washing machines and 'domestic sewage' was excepted in s 14 of the Public Health (Drainage of Trade Premises) Act 1937. It was held that in s 14 'domestic sewage' meant liquid from water closets and baths, lavatories and sanitary conveniences used by workpeople in a factory. Where trade effluent is discharged in breach of conditions contained in a consent, a separate offence under WIA, s 118(5) is committed by each discharge and not by each condition broken, *Severn Trent Water Authority v Express Foods Group Ltd* (1988) *The Times*, 31 October.

The authority may give consent to drain trade effluent into a sewer upon terms which stipulate the volume, temperature, composition and time of day of discharge: it may require that anything which would cause damage to the sewer or make treatment of the sewage more difficult must be extracted (WIA, s 121). In *Re Spenborough Urban District Council's Agreement* [1968] Ch 139 a company made an agreement under s 7 of the 1937 Act with the corporation to discharge effluent but no stipulation was made about ending the agreement. It was held on the construction of the document that either party could determine on reasonable notice and that the 12 months' notice given by the corporation was reasonable.

The question of what is trade effluent can also arise in a planning context in connection with the use of a building 'for treating and disposing of trade waste' (Town and Country Planning General Development Order 1988 (SI No 1813) art 11(1)(*d*), and the Town and Country Planning (Assessment of Environmental Effects) Regulations 1988 (SI No 1199); *R v Rotherham MBC ex p Rankin* [1990] 1 PLR 93).

Where it is desired to discharge 'special category' effluent (defined in WIA, s 138) the undertaker must refer the matter to the Secretary of State. The category covers waste which is prescribed by the 'red list' and is subject to the supervision and control of HM Inspectorate of Pollution under the Trade Effluents (Prescribed Processes and Substances) Regulations 1989 (SI No 1156), Sched 1, or comes under the European Aquatic Environmental Directive (76/464/EEC). The Secretary of State will decide (subject to an appeal under s 122 to the Director) whether discharge is to be permitted and on what terms.

By WRA, s 93 the Secretary of State may by order designate an area as a water protection zone, with a view to preventing or controlling the entry of any polluting mater into controlled waters. By s 94 he may declare nitrate sensitive areas and make agreements with the occupiers to minimise the risk of water pollution by nitrates. By s 85 of the Water Resources Act 1991 (formerly s 107, Water Act 1989) it is an offence to cause or knowingly permit any poisonous, noxious or polluting matter or any solid waste matter to enter any controlled waters. By s 104(1) 'controlled waters' in Pt III of the WRA are of four types: relevant territorial waters; coastal waters; inland waters; and ground waters (any waters contained in underground strata).

Section 85 contains two separate offences of 'causing' and 'knowingly permitting' polluting matter to enter controlled waters. It was held in *Schulmans Incorporated Ltd v National Rivers Authority* (3 December 1991) that constructive knowledge can found the 'knowingly permits' offence. In *Wychavon District Council v NRA* [1992] CLYB 4565 it was held that the council was not liable for 'causing' pollution when it failed to discover promptly the source of a blockage in a sewer which caused discharge of pollution into a river. In Watkins LJ's view it might have been liable for 'knowingly permitting' by inactivity amounting to negligence but this was not charged against it. In *Southern Water Authority v Pegrum* [1989] Crim LR 442 it was held that an authority can be liable for 'causing' pollution even if heavy rain caused a drain to block so that a pig effluent lagoon overflowed. Heavy rain was not so unpredictable as to excuse the defendants, despite their claim that it was an 'Act of God'. In *R v CPC (UK) Ltd* (1994) *The Times*, 4 August CPC bought a factory in which, unknown to them, sub-contractors had previously installed piping with a latent defect. The piping leaked, allowing a caustic liquid to drain into a river. CPC could be liable, since neither fault nor knowledge was needed to found an offence under WRA 1991, s 85(1).

In *National Rivers Authority v Yorkshire Water Services Ltd* [1994] 3 WLR 1202 (HL) an unknown person discharged a trade chemical into trade effluent which passed through the appellants' sewage works and into controlled waters. It was held that they could be convicted under the Water Act 1989, s 107(1) of causing the material to enter controlled waters but on the facts had a defence under s 108(7) as the discharge of the chemical was a breach of a condition of the agreement to receive the trade effluent. The pollutant was discharged at night when no one was on duty at the treatment works and the appellants could not reasonably have been expected to know of its presence, or prevent it (s 108(7)(c)).

It was held in *R v Dovermoss Ltd* (1995) *The Times*, 8 February (CA) that for the purposes of WRA, s 85(1) 'controlled waters', as defined in WRA, ss 104(1)(c) and 221 applied to watercourses such as streams, ditches, and so on, even if such watercourses overflowed or dried up; and that 'pollution' was a matter of fact and degree. If the water was polluted, it was not necessary to establish actual harm; the likelihood of causing harm to animal or plant life or those who used the water was sufficient. A person can be liable for 'causing' polluting matter to enter water even though it escapes without negligence on his part (*Alphacell Ltd v Woodward* [1972] AC 824 (HL) (decided under the Rivers (Prevention of Pollution) Act 1951, s 2), followed in *Price v Cromack* [1975] 1 All ER 113). In *FJH Wrothwell Ltd v Yorkshire Water Authority* (1983) *The Times*, 31 October a director of the defendant company deliberately poured into its drains 12 gallons of a concentrated herbicide known to be toxic to fish, meaning it to discharge in the public sewer. By a system of drainage unknown to him it entered a stream and not the sewer. The company was liable for 'causing' it to flow into the river. The word 'cause' was a simple word in everyday use and must be construed by the exercise of common sense applied to the facts of the case. The company was liable under the Rivers (Prevention of Pollution) Act 1951, s 2 and the Salmon and Fresh Water Fisheries Act 1975, s 4, but not under the Public Health Act 1936, s 27. If a third person interferes with plant or equipment and thereby effluent enters a stream, the owner of the plant is not liable for 'causing' it to do so (*Impress (Worcester) Ltd v Rees* [1971] 2 All ER 357).

In *Attorney-General's Reference (No 1 of 1994)* (1995) *The Times*, 26 January (CA) the first respondent collected and disposed of toxic waste; the second respondent was the sewerage undertaker with statutory duties to provide and maintain sewerage disposal systems; the third respondent was the local borough council performing for profit duties delegated to it by the statutory undertaker. The Court of Appeal answered the referred points of law as follows:

(1) The offence of causing polluting matter to enter controlled waters contrary to s 107(1) of the Water Act 1989 (now WRA 1991, s 85) could be committed by one or more persons where they executed separate acts and the acts contributed to the matter entering the waters.

(2) Where a sewerage company set up and owned a plant or system (as in this case) to carry out its sewerage duties, then if sewerage passing through polluted the waters, the company had participated in an active operation which resulted in pollution and had 'caused' the pollution within s 107 (s 85).

(3) Running a system in an unmaintained state could be sufficient to constitute 'causing'.

(4) The word 'knowingly' was not to be construed as qualifying the word 'causes' in s 107 (s 85).

(5) Mere tacit standing by or looking on was not 'causing'; there must be some active participation.

10 Compulsory acquisition

Where a relevant undertaker finds it necessary to acquire land compulsorily under WIA, ss 155 and 167 for its operations in carrying out its duties it must follow the procedure laid down in the Acquisition of Land Act 1981 and the Compulsory Purchase Act 1965, giving due notice to all the persons with an interest in the land and making advertisements in a local newspaper. The undertaker's powers include a right to create new rights and to extinguish existing ones (WIA, s 155). If there are objectors a public enquiry will be held and the order will require the confirmation of the confirming authority (1981 Act, s 13). In default of agreement the compensation for the land will be assessed by the Lands Tribunal. Compensation is also payable for the severance or injurious affection of other land not compulsorily acquired (Lands Clauses Consolidation Act 1845, s 49; Compulsory Purchase Act 1965, ss 7, 10). For example, in *Russell v Bradfield Rural District Council* (1957) 8 P & CR 432, a plot of land of 0.843 acre was acquired for a sewage works in the centre of a dairy farm of some 86 acres. The Lands Tribunal awarded the following items as compensation at 1957 values: for three unobtrusive manholes which did not interfere with cultivation, £4 each; for a sewer pipe line 313 yards long which might sterilise the land for building purposes for 12 feet on either side but was too deep to interfere with cultivation, £16; for an effluent pipe 209 feet long, £5; for cleansing a stream, £36; for fencing a ditch, £42; for severance and injurious affection of the farm because of the position and smell of the sewage disposal works, £400. Although though it was argued that there are smells on farms anyway, the Tribunal took the view that people do not like sewage works on dairy farms and that their dislike would be reflected in the price that they would pay for the farm. The rules for assessing compensation in every case where land is compulsorily acquired or injuriously affected are laid down in the Land Compensation Act 1961, Pt II, ss 5–16, as supplemented by the Land Compensation Act 1973, ss 44–51.

11 Compensation

By WIA, s 182 it shall be the duty of every relevant undertaker to obtain the approval of the Secretary of State to a code of practice with respect to the exercise of its powers. Breach of the code does not of itself give rise to a right to compensation but the Director General of Water Services may have regard to a breach in deciding whether to give a direction to the undertaker, as part of which he may award conpensation to the claimant (s 182(4)).

Where a sewerage undertaker places a sewer in private land compensation is payable for damage so caused (WIA, s 180 and Sched 12; WRA, s 177 and Sched 21). The authority acquires an interest in land (an easement) and damages are payable for (a) the easement and (b) the damages, present or future, arising from the acquisition, *Thurrock Joint Sewerage Board v Thames Land Co Ltd* (1925) 90 JP 1. The sum paid will include an element for possible future disturbance for maintaining and repair, a 'recognition payment' (*Markland v Cannock Rural District Council* (1973) 227 EG 1173). If damage is done on a future entry compensation will in addition be payable for that damage (*Markland's* case). If the work of laying a sewer is done negligently and subsidence occurs, an action is not statute barred six years after the work was done, under the Limitation Act 1980. Where such an excavation has been made there is a continuing nuisance and a fresh cause of action on each occasion of subsidence, *Crumbie v Wallsend Local Board*, [1891] 1 QB 503, *Smith Stone & Knight Ltd v Birmingham District Council* [1988] EGCS 49. It is no defence for the authority to plead that the works were done negligently and were therefore unauthorised, the authority is liable for the negligence of its sub-contractors, *Marriage v East Norfolk Rivers Catchment Board* [1950] 1 KB 284, *Smith Stone & Knight Ltd* (above).

In assessment, there are four main factors. They are:
(1) The trend of payments for pipe-lines of that type. An oil pipe-line might be less desirable than a sewer, because of the possibility of greater damage from a leak.
(2) Payments for pipe-lines of that type in relation to capital land values. In *Markland's* case there was an award of 25p per linear yard for 1,247 yards for an 11-yard wide easement strip for a 9-inch sewer in farmland, with in addition 11 manholes at £5 each and two at £10 each, a total of £387.

(3) The trend of capital land values.

(4) The trend of payments for other types of pipe-lines.

These principles were enunciated in *Marklands's* case and were followed, in respect of a gas main, in *Wells-Kendrew v British Gas Corporation* (1974) 229 EG 272. In *Lucey's Personal Representatives and Wood v Harrogate Corporation* (1963) 14 P & CR 376, compensation of £75 for a wayleave 466 linear yards long for an 18-inch sewer pipe and 6 manholes in farm land was awarded. If the laying of the sewer has increased the value of the land by more than the loss which the laying has caused, no compensation is payable. The gain is set off against the loss, but the owner of the land does not seem to be liable to pay the water authority for any gain to him (1936 Act, s 278(4)). In *Rush & Tomkins Ltd v West Kent Sewerage Board* (1963) 14 P & CR 469, a compensation figure of £1,480 for laying a sewer was cancelled out by enhancement of value of part of the applicant's land by the sum of £3,800 because construction of the sewer made the land more readily saleable as industrial land. No compensating sum was claimed from the owner.

In *Collins v Thames Water Utilities Ltd* (1994) 9449 EG 116 (Lands Tribunal) a sewer was laid at a depth of 700mm across the bottom of the garden of a private house, with a protected area of 6m, amounting to some 36 per cent of the garden. Previously the house was served by a septic tank but was now connected to the new sewer (which served 420 houses). Compensation was awarded of £415 for entry, disturbance and claimants' time but nothing was awarded for injurious affection to the property as the enhancement in utility and value meant that there was no detrimental effect, even though there was a right of future entry and a protected area.

In relation to compensation for pipe laying, matters to be considered include payments for a sewer easement the payment for which is in practice assessed on so much a metre of run, based on 50 per cent of the vacant possession value of a notional easement strip. In a helpful booklet, *Wayleaves and Easement*, (Country Landowners Association (W3/1989)) it is suggested that the easement strip needed to protect the pipe should vary from 20 feet to 80 feet, depending on the diameter of the pipe-line; for example, 20 feet for 24 inches and below, up to 80 feet for 48 inches. In addition to payment for an easement there should be a claim for compensation for manholes, valves and other structures whether or not above ground. Under a national agreement made in 1989

British Telecom pay an annual wayleave of £12.66 for an above ground manhole, for loss to agricultural operations. The laying of the pipe will cause damage, disturbance and loss of profits and professional fees for negotiating all the matters may also be claimed. The British Standards publication, BS 8010: *Pipelines on Land: General*, should also be consulted.

In *Donovan v Dwr Cymru—Welsh Water Plc and Another* [1994] 1 EGLR 203 (Lands Tribunal) it was held that where contractors for Welsh Water had laid a sewer outside the line notified to the owner by a notice of entry under the Water Act 1989, s 153 the Lands Tribunal had jurisdiction. This was a 'relevant pipe' and work was done on 'relevant land' under Sched 19, paras 4 and 6 of the Act. The laying was attributable to the exercise of the statutory powers in the Act. Any dispute with the contractors was for Welsh Water to resolve.

In *Jordan v Norfolk County Council* [1994] 4 All ER 218 the council laid a sewage pipe through the plaintiff's land without his agreement, cutting down many trees. He obtained a mandatory injunction against them to remove the pipe and restore the land 'so far as reasonably practicable' and to pay £25,000 damages. A tree-planting scheme proposed would have cost £230–300,000 but the site was worth only £25,000. The court ordered a new scheme, limiting it to a reasonable cost with regard to the nature of the site.

Chapter 8

Land Drainage

The Land Drainage Act 1991 ('LDA') is based primarily on the Land Drainage Act 1976 and the Water Act 1989. It concerns the internal drainage boards and their powers and the land drainage powers of local authorities. The National Rivers Authority ('NRA') exercises control over internal drainage boards and may exercise concurrent land drainage powers with the boards. Environmental duties also govern the exercise of the powers.

The National Rivers Authority and the London Waste Regulation Authority were abolished by s 2(3) of the Environment Act 1995 and their property, rights and liabilities were transferred to the Environment Agency on the transfer date. This chapter should be read accordingly.

By LDA, s 1 there shall continue to be districts, known as internal drainage districts, which shall be such areas as will derive benefit from drainage operations; and boards, known as internal drainage boards, which shall be the drainage board for the district. By s 4 the NPA may be made a drainage board by the Minister of Agriculture, Fisheries and Food (defined in s 72).

1 Powers of authorities

The drainage board of each area has powers to cleanse, repair or otherwise maintain in an efficient state any watercourse or drainage work; to improve any existing watercourses or drainage work, such as by widening, deepening, straightening, removing or altering any obstruction such as a dam or weir; and to construct new works such as watercourses required for the drainage of the area (LDA, s 14(2)).

The term 'watercourses' includes all rivers, streams, ditches,

117

drains, cuts, culverts, dykes, sluices, sewers and passages through which water flows (LDA, s 72(1)).

Where in the opinion of the drainage board or local authority the proper flow of water in a watercourse is impeded, either may serve notice on the person in occupation or control of the land adjoining the obstruction or the person responsible for causing it, requiring him to remedy it (LDA, s 25). An appeal against the notice can be made to the magistrates within 21 days of the service of the notice (LDA, s 27(1)).

A person may not obstruct the flow of any watercourse such as by a dam, weir or culvert without the permission in writing (not to be unreasonably withheld) of the drainage authority, or alter any obstruction in a watercourse without permission (LDA, s 23(1)(e)). If he does so he is deemed to have created a nuisance which he may by notice be ordered to abate within a specified time (LDA, s 24(1)).

A person may not without the consent of the NRA erect any structure in, over or under a watercourse which is part of a main river or alter or repair any such structure if the work is likely to impede the flow of water or impede any drainage work (WRA, s 109).

A drainage or local authority can deposit on the bank of a watercourse or on land adjoining it any matter removed from the watercourse in the process of dredging, widening or deepening it, unless a statutory nuisance within the meaning of the Environmental Protection Act 1990, Pt III, would be caused by so doing (LDA, s 15(1)–(3)). Where a person suffers damage by such depositing, the authority may compensate him if it thinks fit, but where he suffers damage which the authority could by taking reasonable care have avoided doing it must compensate him (s 15(4)). He cannot claim damages, as distinct from compensation, unless he can show negligence in the manner of carrying out the work. In *Marriage v East Norfolk Rivers Catchment Board* [1950] 1 KB 284, the (then) board dredged a river and deposited the dredgings on one bank. This prevented flood water from escaping over the bank, so the water went into another channel in abnormal quantity and carried away the plaintiff's bridge. He failed in a claim based on nuisance and negligence to show negligence in the manner of carrying out the work, and was therefore limited to the compensation provided for by statute. The powers of the authorities are permissive. If they fail to exercise their powers at all or exercise them honestly but ineffectively, they are not liable for damage sustained by reason of the failure or partial failure to exercise (*East Suffolk Rivers Catchment Board v Kent* [1941] AC 74). If the authority is under a duty to act, as distinct from having merely a power to act, it is a question of construction whether an individual affected has a remedy in tort. For example, the provision in the statute of a remedy may exclude any action in tort. In *Hesketh v Birmingham Corporation* [1924] 1 KB 260 the corporation owned a sewer which ran alongside a natural stream and at times of heavy rain outlets relieved pressure on the sewer by discharge into the stream. Because of building on neighbouring land, in the course of time the outlets became inadequate and after a heavy storm the land became flooded. Held: no action would lie for negligence for failure to enlarge the capacity of the stream, the remedy lay under s 299 of the Public Health Act 1875 with assessment of compensation by arbitration under s 308. It was held in *Dear v Thames Water* (1994) 33 Con LR 43 that a statutory authority may be liable for negligence or nuisance if damage is caused to an individual's property as a result either of a negligent act on the part of the authority or of its having created a nuisance, subject to any express or implied defence. The duty to exercise statutory powers is owed to the public at large and not to any particular member of it. (Authority held not liable to a householder when foul and storm water damaged his house when the water backed up because of inadequate culvert.)

2 Protection of the environment

By a new Pt IVA inserted into the Land Drainage Act 1991 by s 1 of the Land Drainage Act 1994 it shall be the duty of an internal drainage board, of each of the relevant Ministers and of the National Rivers Authority so to exercise any of their powers as to further the conservation and enhancement of the natural beauty and flora, fauna and geological or physiographical features of special interest, making a new LDA 1991, s 61A(1). Also by s 61A(1) the authorities must have regard to the desirability of protecting and conserving buildings, sites and objects of archeological, architectural or historic interest; and to take into account any effect which the proposals would have on the beauty or amenity of any rural or urban area or any flora, fauna, features, buildings, sites or objects. By a new s 61B there are similar duties placed on local authorities. The Ministers may approve codes of practice giving practical guidance on these matters to internal drainage boards and local authorities (s 61E).

3 Drainage of another's land

Where a ditch (whether open, culverted or piped) (LDA, s 28(5)) is in such a condition as to cause injury to any land or to prevent the improvement of drainage, the Agricultural Land Tribunal may order any person named in the orders to carrry out such work for putting it into proper condition as may be stated in the order (s 28(1)). If within three months the work is not done the Minister of Agriculture or any drainage board authorised by the Minister may enter on the land, do the work and recover from the person named any expenses so incurred (s 29(2)). There are similar provisions where the drainage of land requires work on a ditch on 'other' land (s 30(1)). The Agricultural Land Tribunal may authorise an applicant to enter the other land to carry out the specified work. By s 39(5) where any person sustains injury by reason of the exercise of any power conferred by s 29 he is entitled to compensation, to be assessed by the Lands Tribunal in a disputed case, unless the power was exercised for the purpose of executing works which the person was required to do by an order made under s 28.

4 Byelaws

Internal drainage boards or local authorities (except a county council) have power to make such byelaws as they consider necessary to secure the efficient working of the drainage system in the area (LDA, s 66(1)). They may in particular prevent the discharge into the watercourse of matter likely to obstruct it, and prevent the improper use of the watercourse or its banks to preserve it from damage (s 66(2)). Byelaws made under the power do not take effect until confirmed by the Minister of Agriculture.

5 Compulsory acquisition

An internal drainage board may acquire land compulsorily for its statutory purposes, and by agreement (LDA, s 62(1)). It may secure the creation of new interests in or over land (s 62(4)). It is likely that the term 'new interests or rights' is wider than an interest with the characteristics of a common law easement; a statutory right derives its validity from statute and not from the common law principles. There may, for example, be no dominant tenement which the drainage right benefits. The procedure to be followed is that under the Acquisition of Land Act 1981 (s 146(4)).

6 Compensation

Where a person suffers damage or loss because of the exercise by a drainage authority of its general powers he can (except where otherwise provided) claim compensation, to be assessed by the Lands Tribunal if agreement cannot be reached (LDA, s 62(5)). In *Glazebrook v Gwynedd River Board* (1964) 15 P & CR 75, the board carried out drainage works in a stream running through the claimant's dairy farm. He alleged that this reduced the amount of drinking water for his cattle, but as it was held on the facts that the benefit to his land by the drainage exceeded any loss no compensation was awarded. In *Welsh National Water Development Authority v Burgess* (1974) 28 P & CR 378 (CA), a person with fishing rights on a river was awarded £700 damages for diminution of the value of the fishing when the water authority's predecessor (the Gwynedd River Authority) 'retrained' the river, so as to avoid further flooding after two heavy floods had caused substantial deposits of gravel in the river. The works, though necessary, were too drastic and paid no adequate regard to the fishing interests.

Chapter 9

The Environment Act 1995

1 Introduction

The Environment Act 1995 ('EA 1995') includes the following objects in its short title: to set up a body corporate known as the Environment Agency (and a similar body for Scotland ('SEPA')); to transfer functions to it from other bodies; to make provision for contaminated land and abandoned mines; to make further provision for National Parks; the control of pollution, the conservation of natural resources and the environment.

Section 1 establishes the Environment Agency ('the Agency') of between 8 and 15 members and by s 2(1) on the transfer date the functions of the National Rivers Authority, of waste regulation authorities, of disposal authorities, of HM Inspectorate of Pollution and some of the functions of the Secretary of State under the Radioactive Substances Act 1993 and the Water Industry Act 1991 in relation to special category effluent, are transferred to the Agency.

By s 2(3) the National Rivers Authority and the London Waste Regulation Authority are abolished and by s 3(1) their property, rights and liabilities vest in the Agency on the transfer date. Waste regulation authorities must make a scheme under which appropriate parts of their property, rights and liabilities are transferred to the Agency (s 3(3)).

The Ministers shall from time to time give guidance to the Agency with regard to aims and objectives which they consider appropriate to be followed (s 4(1)) and the Agency shall exercise its pollution control powers to prevent or minimise pollution of the environment (s 5(1)) and with respect to water to enhance natural beauty, conserve flora and fauna and use waters and land for recreational purposes (s 6(1)). By s 9 the Ministers are empow-

ered to approve codes of practice for giving practical guidance to
the Agency with respect to matters concerning their water duties
(s 6), their general environmental and recreational duties (s 7) and
their environmental duties with regard to sites of special interest
(s 8).

2 Powers

By s 35(1) each new Agency may do anything which, in its
opinion, is calculated to facilitate, or is conducive or incidental to,
carrying out its functions. It may acquire and dispose of land
and other property and carry out such engineering or building
operations as it considers appropriate. By s 10(3) it may join with
or act on behalf of water or sewerage undertakers in carrying out
works or acquiring land. The normal acquisition procedures and
compensation provisions will apply. By s 37(1), in considering
whether to exercise any power conferred upon it, the Agency
shall, unless it is unreasonable to do so, take into account the
costs likely to be incurred, and the benefits which are likely to
accrue, in consequence of the exercise or non-exercise of the
power. By s 37(2) this duty does not affect the Agency's obligation
to discharge any duties or meet any aims or objectives imposed
upon it otherwise than under s 37.

Chapter 10

Electricity

1 General background

The Electricity Act 1989 ('EA') had the effect of privatising the electricity industry in England, Wales and Scotland (but except for certain sections it does not apply to Northern Ireland, s 113(3)). The Central Electricity Generating Board was split into two new generating companies (PowerGen and National Power) and was required to make a scheme for the division of all its property, rights and liabilities between the two generating companies and a transmission company (the National Grid Company, which has the monopoly of high voltage electricity transmission). By the Area Boards (Dissolution) Order 1993 (SI No 2825), from 10 December 1993 each of the twelve Area Boards had its property transferred to new supply companies nominated by the Secretary (s 65) and in the case of the Scottish Boards their property was transferred to nominated companies of which two were designated as the Scottish electricity companies and one as the Scottish nuclear company. The system of regulation of generation, transmission and supply is in the hands of the Director General of Electricity Supply who has the functions of carrying out his duties in the way best calculated to promote competition in the supply and generation of electricity, to secure that all reasonable demands for electricity are satisfied, and to protect consumers' interests (s 3); some of these duties are exercised either by the Director or the Secretary of State (s 3(2), (3)). The Director establishes consumers' committees for each area (s 2, Sched 2); their functions are defined in ss 51 and 52. The Director, in consultation with the Secretary of State, deals with the issue of licences to generate and transmit (see below).

The Competition and Service (Utilities) Act 1992 gives effect to a government commitment contained in the Citizen's Charter (HMSO, Cm 1599) to give the Directors General for water, gas, electricity and telecommunications further legal powers to ensure that better services are provided for consumers. For each utility the Act provides for the Directors to make regulations for standards of performance, to collect information on levels of performance and make it available, to establish procedures for dealing with consumers' complaints, to determine disputes, including those on billing and (where relevant) to prevent disconnections in cases where there is genuinely a dispute. This provision will not apply where disputing the bill is a tactic to avoid payment, *Jones v East Ham Corporation* [1935] 1 KB 367. Under the Electricity (Standards of Performance) Regulations 1991 (SI No 1344/91) compensation is automatically made to the consumer for failure to meet stipulated standards of performance; a tariff of compensation is given in the Regulations. There are exemptions for such matters as severe weather and failure to gain admission to premises.

2 Generation of electricity

It shall be the duty of a public electricity supplier to develop and maintain an efficient, co-ordinated and economical system of electricity supply (s 9(1)).

It is an offence to generate electricity for the purpose of giving a supply of electricity to any premises or enabling a supply to be given, or to transmit electricity for that purpose, or to supply it to any premises, without a licence or an exemption from licensing (s 4(1)). 'Supply' in relation to electricity means supply through electric lines otherwise than to premises occupied by a licence holder for the purpose of carrying on his authorised activities; and 'transmit' means transmit by means of a system of high voltage lines and electrical plant used for conveying electricity from a generating station to a substation (s 4(4)). Exemption may be granted from the need to have a licence for generation or supply but not from the need to have one for transmission (s 5(1), (2)). Licences may include such conditions as appear to the grantor to be requisite and in particular may require the licence holder to enter into agreements for the use of his lines and plant by private electricity suppliers (s 7). Licences may be modified by agreement (s 11) and the Director may make reference to the Monopolies Commission for consideration whether any matters relating to the generation, transmission or supply under a licence operate or may be expected to operate against the public interest (s 12).

By s 36(1) a generating station shall not be constructed, extended or operated except in accordance with a consent granted by the Secretary of State except where the permitted capacity does not exceed 50 megawatts or such other capacity as the Secretary stipulates (s 36(2)). Consent is also required for the installation of overhead lines unless within the premises of the installer or of a nominal voltage not exceeding 20 kilovolts (s 37(1), (2)).

It shall be the duty of the holder of a licence authorising him to transmit electricity to develop and maintain an efficient, co-ordinated and economical system of transmission and to facilitate competition in the supply and generation of electricity (s 9(2)).

3 Supply

A public electricity supplier (PES) is a person who is authorised by a licence under s 6(1)(c) to supply electricity to any premises in his authorised area (s 6(9)). It is the duty of a PES to develop and maintain an efficient, co-ordinated and economical system of electricity supply (s 9(1)). A PES shall, subject to the Act and regulations, upon being required to do so by the owner or occupier of any premises, give a supply of electricity to those premises and so far as may be necessary for that purpose, provide electric lines or electric plant or both (s 16(1)). A person requiring a supply shall give due notice and as soon as practicable thereafter the PES shall give him notice stating the extent to which the request is acceptable, the prices to be charged, the payment or security required and any restrictions which must be imposed under regulations made under s 29 (which relate to supply and safety) (s 16(2), (4)). There is no duty to supply if there is a supply being given to the premises by a private electricity supplier (s 17(1)). The Director will determine any dispute (s 23(1)).

A 'squatter' in premises is not entitled to demand a supply under s 16: *Woodcock v South Western Electricity Board* [1975] 1 WLR 152. The statutory liability is to supply electricity. A board is not liable if loss or damage is caused because the supply is irregular or fluctuating, unless it makes a collateral contract with the consumer that the supply will at all times be adequate for a stated purpose (such as to keep infra-red lamps at a certain temperature so that chicks will not suffer: *Willmore v South Eastern Electricity Board* [1957] 2 Lloyd's Rep 375; in this case the claim failed, there being no collateral contract, although the board made many attempts to regularise the supply, knowing that chicks were being kept).

The Public Electricity Supply Code is contained in Sched 6 and deals with: the recovery of electricity charges; the restoration of supply after it has been cut off as a result of a default by a tariff customer; the offence of restoring the supply without consent; the intentional or culpably negligent damage of electrical plant; powers of entry by authorised officers of the PES for inspection, discontinuance, replacing or repair; duties of officers to safeguard the premises after authorised entry.

By s 19(1) where any electric line or electrical plant is provided by a PES in pursuance of s 16(1) the supplier may require any expenses reasonably incurred to be defrayed by the person requiring the supply, to such extent as is reasonable in the circumstances. The reference to 'expenses reasonably incurred' includes also a reference to the capitalised value of any expenses likely to be incurred by the supplier in maintaining the line or plant in the future in so far as they will not be recoverable by the supplier as part of the charges made by him for the supply (s 18(4)). The Secretary of State may, after consultation with the Director, make regulations for entitling the supplier to claim expenses reasonably incurred in providing a line or plant (s 19(2)). A person who requires a supply of electricity may enter into an agreement for it where the maximum power to be made available exceeds ten megawatts or such other wattage as the Secretary of State may by order specify and it is otherwise reasonable in all the circumstances for such an agreement to be entered into; the Secretary of State must first consult with public electricity suppliers and others appearing to him to be representative of persons likely to be affected (s 22(1), (2)). The Director determines disputes under ss 16–21 between a PES and a person requiring a supply of electricity (s 22(1)).

By Sched 7, cl 1, where a customer of an electricity supplier is to be charged wholly or partly for a supply by reference to the quantity of electricity supplied, the supply shall be given through a meter supplied by the electricity supplier (or if agreed, by the customer). Meters are to be certified by meter examiners appointed by the Director (para 4(1), (5)) and it shall be the duty of the meter examiner to examine and test any meter at the request of the customer (para 7). It is a criminal offence (summary conviction can bring a fine not exceeding level 3) if any person intentionally or by culpable negligence alters the register which records the quantity of electricity supplied or prevents the meter from registering the quantity (para 11(1)).

4 Powers of licence holders

The Electricity Act 1989, s 10(1) provides that Scheds 3 and 4 (which relate to compulsory acquisition and other powers) shall have effect in relation to a PES or a person authorised by licence to transmit electricity and, to the extent that the licence so provides, in relation to any other licence holder.

Acquisition

By Sched 3, para 1(1) the Secretary of State may authorise a licence holder to purchase compulsorily any land required for any purpose connected with the carrying on of the activities authorised by the licence. By para 1(2) 'land' includes 'any right over land (other than, in Scotland, a right to abstract, divert and use water); and the power of the Secretary of State under this paragraph includes power to authorise the acquisition of rights over land by creating new rights as well as acquiring existing ones'. A consent to acquire which is not acted on within six months of the day that it is granted ceases to have effect (para 1(4)). Where a licence holder has acquired land under para 1 he shall not dispose of it or of any interest in it without the consent of the Director (para 1(5)). By Pt II of Sched 3 the procedure on acquisition is that applicable under the Acquisition of Land Act 1981 (para 5(1)) and paras 6–14 give appropriate adaptations of the Compulsory Purchase Act 1965 to enable new rights to be acquired.

Street works

Schedule 4 confers other powers on licence holders. By para 1 a licence holder may: install works under, over, in, on, along, or across any street and from time to time inspect, maintain, adjust, repair, alter, replace or remove any electric lines or plant and any structures for housing or covering any such lines or plant. For those purposes the licence holder may open and break up any street or any sewers, drains or tunnels within or under any street, or tunnel or bore under any street or remove or use all earth and materials under any street (para 1(1)). By a proviso to para 1 he may not 'place any electric line or electric plant into, through or against any building, or in any land not dedicated to public use'. The power to place on or over a street shall be exercisable only with the consent of the highway authority (in the case of a publicly maintainable street), or with the consent of the railway or navigation authority (where the street is under the control of one of them), or, if the street does not fall under one of them but is repairable by a person, with the consent of that person (para 1(2)). In all three cases the consent is not to be unreasonably withheld (para 1(2)). A licence holder shall do as little damage as possible in exercising his powers under para 1 and shall make compensation for any damage done in exercise of them (para 1(6)). He shall so exercise his powers as to secure that nothing which he installs or keeps installed under, over, in, on, along or across any street becomes a source of danger to the public (para 1(7)).

A licence holder may execute works under paras 1 or 2 notwithstanding that they involve a temporary or permanent alteration to: any electric line or electric plant under the control of another licence holder; any gas pipe under the control of a public gas supplier; any water pipe under the control of a person supplying water under the exercise of statutory powers; or any telecommunication apparatus operated by a person to whom the telecommunications code applies. The licence holder must give to the 'relevant undertaker' not less than one month's notice of the proposed work and the time and place of it (para 3(3)), except in case of an emergency (para 3(4)), and the relevant undertaker may within seven days give a counter-notice saying that he intends to do the necessary works or that they must be done under his supervision; he can charge the licence holder with the expenses if he does the work himself (paras 3(5), (6)). Any public gas supplier, water supplier under statutory powers or public telecommunications operator who is authorised to execute works corresponding to those authorised by paras 1 or 2 may carry out his authorised works notwithstanding that they involve a temporary or permanent alteration to any electric line or electrical plant under the control of a licence holder (para 4(1)).

If damage is caused to electricity apparatus laid in a street by traffic of excessive weight, the authority may claim compensation for the loss from the person responsible for the traffic (*Chichester Corporation v Foster* [1906] 1 KB 167: where a traction engine weighing upwards of ten tons and drawing three trucks fractured a water main which had been sufficiently strong to withstand reasonable traffic for more than 30 years, the owner of the traction engine was held liable for the damage).

Where a statutory undertaker causes a nuisance which is attributable to its carrying out of street works under statutory power, the authority is not liable, unless it has also been negligent (*Department of Transport v North West Water Authority* [1983] 3 WLR 707 (HL), construing Public Utilities Street Works Act 1950, s 18(2)).

Wayleaves, lines and generating stations

By EA, Sched 4, para 6, if it is necessary or expedient for a licence holder in connection with carrying out his authorised activities to install and keep installed an electric line on, under or over any land he may serve notice to that effect on the owner or occupier of the land. If the owner or occupier has failed within the period specified in the notice (not being less than 21 days) to give consent, or has given it on terms to which the licence holder objects the licence holder may apply to the Secretary of State who can grant the wayleave on such terms and conditions as he thinks fit, after affording the owner or occupier an opportunity to be heard (paras 6(4), (5)). A necessary wayleave granted under para 6 shall bind any person who is at any time the owner or occupier of the land (para 6(6)(b)). If the wayleave is determined (for example, by the effluxion of the time for which it was granted) the owner or occupier of the land may give notice to remove the electric line but the licence holder need not comply if he either applies for a wayleave under para 6 or applies for an order for compulsory acquisition of the land (para 8(3)); otherwise he must remove the line within 3 months from the date of the notice (para 8(3)). There is an appeal to the Secretary of State (para 8(4), (5)).

By EA, s 37 an electric line shall not be installed or kept installed above ground except in accordance with a consent granted by the Secretary of State. This does not apply to a line with a nominal voltage not exceeding 20 kilovolts supplying a single consumer or to so much of an electricity line as is within premises. Certain overhead lines are exempted from the requirement for a Secretary of State's consent, by the Overhead Lines (Exemption) Regulations 1990 (SI No 2035) and 1992 (SI No 3074). By s 36 a similar consent is needed for the construction, extension or operation of a generating station exceeding 50 megawatts. Schedule 8 applies to applications under ss 36 and 37. Paragraph 2 of Sched 8 says that a public enquiry shall be held where the local planning authority object to the Minister. Regulations provide that notice of such application shall be published. Schedule 8, para 4 deals with public enquiries, which are governed by the Electricity Generating Stations and Overhead lines (Enquiries Procedure) Rules 1990 (SI No 528).

Planning permission is also needed unless granted by the General Development Order 1988. Express planning permission is not needed for the laying underground of pipes, cables and other apparatus, and the installation of service lines to individual consumers from an electric line, as these matters fall within the general permission given by the Town and Country Planning General Development Order 1988 (SI No 1813, in force from 5 December 1988) Sched 2, Pt 17, Class G. By the conditions attached by Class G2 notice of certain operations must be given to the responsible specified authority before operations commence.

Express planning permission is required for the construction, enlargement or extension of a generating station, unless it was within the small area of permissions in Sched 2, Pt 8, Class A or B.

Environmental assessment

By the Electricity and Pipe-line Works (Assessment of Environmental Effects) Regulations 1990 (SI No 442), on any application under EA, ss 36 or 37 an environmental statement may be required by the Secretary of State to construct or extend a generating station, or install or keep installed an electric line above ground. It will be required on an application for the granting of permission for any new power station of more than 300 MW thermal capacity. The Secretary of State may also call for such an assessment in relation to power stations of less than this capacity and for combined Heat and Power (CHP) or hydro schemes and overhead lines proposed by the CEGB or Area boards. The planning authority's views will be taken fully into account; see also DOE circular 34/76 (Welsh Office 45/76) on 'Procedure for consultation and consent for new electricity generating stations and overhead lines'. The Secretary of State will supply copies to interested bodies and allow representations to be made. The statement must show the likely significant effects of the development on human beings, flora, fauna, soil, water, air, climate and the cultural heritage, and must state the measures to be taken to avoid, reduce or remedy the effect.

Felling and lopping trees

Paragraph 9(1) of Sched 4 applies where any tree is or will be in such close proximity to an electric line or electrical plant which is kept installed or is being or is to be installed by a licence holder as to obstruct or interfere with its installation, maintenance or working or as to constitute an unacceptable source of danger (whether to children or to any other persons). In such a case the licence holder may give notice to the occupier of the land requiring him to fell or lop the tree or cut back its roots so as to prevent it from having the effect mentioned above, subject to the licence holder paying the expenses reasonably incurred in so doing (para 9(1), (2)). If within 21 days of the giving of such a notice the owner or occupier gives a counter-notice objecting to the requirements of the notice the matter shall be referred to the Secretary of State if the counter-notice is not withdrawn (para 9(5)). On such reference the Secretary of State may empower felling or lopping or cutting back of roots to be done and may determine the question of the expenses (para 9(6)). Where the licence holder exercises powers under para 9(4) or (6) he must cause trees to be felled or lopped or their roots to be cut back in accordance with good arboricultural practice so as to do as little damage as possible to the tree and other trees, hedges, fences and crops; he must cause the cuttings to be removed as the owner or occupier may direct and he must make good any damage to the land (para 9(7)). In para 9 'tree' includes any shrub (para 9(8)). It is an offence for any person intentionally to obstruct a person acting in the exercise of any power conferred by paras 9 and 10 (entry on land for purposes of exploration and survey) (para 11(1)).

Compensation

The provisions as to compensation for acquisition of land and rights over land are found in the Acquisition of Land Act 1981 and the Compulsory Purchase Act 1965, as adapted by Sched 3, Pt II of the Electricity Act 1989. Basic scales of compensation for interference with the farming and cultivation of land, and of rental (which can be annual or in a lump sum) for poles and towers, have been agreed by the National Farmers' Union and the Country

Landowners' Association with the National Grid Company and regional electricity companies. The current agreed scale of payments for electricity wayleaves, negotiated between the Country Landowners' Association, the National Farmers' Union and the Electricity Supply Industry, runs from 1 June 1993 and may be found in CLA publication *Cables and Wires* (W3/93). Larger sums are paid for interference with commercial fruit growing than for interference with pasture. British Telecom (and presumably other licensed operators) has agreed to pay the same rates as the electricity industry.

If there is a possibility that future development of the land may be curtailed by the lines, such as by reducing the number of houses which can be built on it when planning permission for residential development is obtained, provision should be made in the wayleave agreement for compensation in the future when this loss becomes apparent. In *Christian Salvesen Ltd v CEGB* (1984) 48 P & CR 465 it was held on the facts that a payment of £900 in 1966 for a wayleave easement for an overhead line and five pylons precluded the payment of later compensation when successors in title to the land were refused planning permission for residential development on the land by reason of the existence of the overhead line. The rights of the parties concerning compensation were governed exclusively by the deed. A similar case was *Mayclose v CEGB* [1987] 2 EGLR 18 where a deed of grant made by landowners with the CEGB provided for rent for wayleaves and also compensation for any diminution in the value of any land for which planning permission had been granted, by reason of the existence of overhead lines. A possible sterilisation of part of the land was envisaged but what happened was that a complete refusal of planning permission was issued. It was held that the owners could not have any more compensation, the deed was made after lengthy negotiations and was intended to encompass the whole of the relationship between the parties, including depreciation in value of the subject land. See also *Allen v South Eastern Electricity Board* [1988] 1 EGLR 171 (CA) where it was held on the facts that the phrase in a deed of compensation 'cannot take full advantage of the said planning permission' did not mean 'cannot sell the property for as high a price as could have been obtained but for the rights granted to the board'. The compensation provision was directed to such consequences as a restriction on the density of development attributable to the existence of pylons and cables. The appellant was not prevented from taking 'full advantage' of the planning permissions.

In view of these cases it would be wise for an owner to reserve carefully and unequivocally his right to future compensation (see a standard deed negotiated by the CLA and the NFU concerning gas pipe-lines). The boards will also pay for any injurious affection where trees have to be felled to make way for the wires, where land has to be left uncultivated because of them, or where minerals have to be left unworked because of the pylons. If lines prevent or impede the aerial spraying of crops, with increased expense for ground treatment, a claim can be made for this additional expense: *Pryor v Central Electricity Generating Board* (1968) 206 EG 1143 (£700 awarded on this account).

In *Clouds Estate Trustees v Southern Electricity Board* (Ref 183/ 1982) (1983) 268 EG 367 and 451 the annual rent paid under wayleave consents for overhead lines was assessed from 1 January 1982 at 50p per single pole, 50p per stay or strut, 75p per H pole and 25p per earthwire. The rent for underground cables was to be 15p per 25m run of cable and multiples of 25p and 30p per 50m run. Because of the permanency of the structures the assessment was effectively one by consent for the compulsory acquisition of rights over the land, despite the use of the term 'rent'. The land commanded the highest agricultural rents of any county in England, being in Wiltshire, and the award should not be taken as fixing a norm. The figures in use in 1987 included: 51p annually for a pole; 17p per 25 metres of cable, with much higher figures for interference with agricultural operations (arable £6.48 for a pole, £7.88 for a stay or strut).

Benefits attributable to the work can be set off against claims by the owner. In *Collins v Thames Water Utilities Ltd* (1994) 9449 EG 116 (Lands Tribunal) a sewer was laid under the Water Industry Act 1991, Sched 12, across the foot of the garden of a private house at a depth of 700mm, with a protected area of 6m, amounting to 36 per cent of the garden. The house was then connected to the new sewer together with 419 other houses and the septic tank which had served it was not needed. Compensation of £415 was awarded for entry, disturbance and claimants' time. Nothing was payable for alleged injurious affection, any detriment in future was negligible and the enhancement of the property's drainage must be set off against it.

In *Jordan v Norfolk County Council* [1994] 4 All ER 218 the council laid a sewer through a person's land without his consent, cutting down many trees. He obtained a mandatory injunction to remove the sewer and restore the site so far as reasonably practicable, including a tree-planting scheme of reasonable cost, and £25,000 damages.

Chapter 11

Gas

The Gas Act 1986 ('1986 Act') privatised the British Gas Corporation. It provided for the issue of shares in a new company, British Gas plc, and for the vesting in this company of the property, rights and liabilities of the British Gas Corporation from 24 August 1986 (s 49). The BGC was dissolved by s 57 on 28 February 1990 (SI No 147). The former monopoly position of BGC as a supplier of gas was abolished (s 3) and gas may now be supplied by any 'public gas supplier' (PGS) who holds an authorisation under s 7, or anyone authorised by the Secretary of State, s 8. It is an offence to supply gas through pipes to any premises unless the supplier is authorised under ss 7 or 8 or comes within the exceptions set out in s 6 (ss 5 and 6A as substituted for s 5 by the Gas (Exempt Supplies) Act 1993, ss 1 and 2). A Director General of Gas Supply ('the Director') is appointed by the Secretary of State to perform the functions assigned to him by ss 4 and 34–38 (as amended by the Competition and Service (Utilities) Act 1992, s 56(6) and Sched 1) (hereafter called the '1992 Act') (1986 Act, s 1). His functions include protecting the interests of consumers and protecting the public from dangers arising from the transmission of gas through pipes (s 4). A Gas Consumers' Council replaces the national and regional Gas Consumers' Councils (1986 Act, ss 2, 4, 41 and Sched 2).

Under the 1986 Act it is the duty of a PGS to develop and maintain an efficient, co-ordinated and economical system of gas supply (s 9), and to avoid any undue preference in the supply of gas to persons entitled to a supply under s 10 (below). Subsequent references in this chapter are to the 1986 Act unless otherwise stated.

By the 1992 Act, s 11, inserting new ss 33A and 33B into the 1986 Act, the Director may make regulations prescribing standards of supply by a PGS and standards of performance. Compensation may be claimed by a consumer who is affected by failure to meet a prescribed standard, 1992 Act, s 33A(4); payment is not automatic, cp electricity supply.

1 Duty to supply

An owner or occupier may require from a PGS a supply of gas to any premises which are within 25 yards of a relevant main of the supplier or are connected by a service pipe to such main (s 10(1)) and in the former case the PGS shall also provide and lay any necessary pipe but the PGS is not under an obligation to supply to any premises gas in excess of 25,000 therms in any period of twelve months (s 10(5)). No PGS can be required to give or continue a supply if prevented by circumstances beyond its control, or if there could be danger to the public by so doing (s 10(6)). If a PGS agrees to supply more than 25,000 therms yearly to any premises it may do so by special contract (s 10(7)).

The cost of providing and laying any pipe falls upon the person requiring the supply under s 10(1) to the extent that it runs over his land or, to the extent that it does not run over his land, that it exceeds a distance of 30 feet from the main (s 10(3)). These dimensions in yards and feet have been amended by the Gas (Metrication) Regulations 1992 from 1 April 1992 (SI No 450). The Regulations are made under the European Communities Act 1972, s 2(2)–(4).

The PGS is under a duty to maintain, repair or renew the pipe at the reasonable expense of the owner or occupier (Sched 5, para 1). A person requiring a supply must give reasonable notice to the PGS and if so required give security for payment of expenses, ss 10(2), 11. The PGS's obligation to supply does not extend beyond a supply for domestic purposes or lighting if the capacity of the main is insufficient to supply gas for any other purpose, s 10(7). But if a person requiring a supply for some other purpose, such as an industrial one, contracts with the PGS so as to justify the PGS laying down the mains or other apparatus for the larger supply, then the person will become entitled to a supply, s 10(7).

Where the supply of gas to premises is cut off or is likely to be cut off for failure to pay for the supply the local authority may, at the request in writing of the occupier, make an arrangement with the PGS for restoration or continuance of the supply on agreed terms, Local Government (Miscellaneous Provisions) Act 1976, s 33 (as amended).

Section 15 and Sched 5 contain the Public Gas Supply Code now slightly amended by ss 19 and 53 of the Competition and Service (Utilities) Act 1992 (see below). In addition to the matters already mentioned it deals with meters, (paras 3–6), improper use of gas and injury to gas fittings (paras 9–11), the duty of a PGS to prevent escapes of gas (para 13), and entry onto premises to inspect, discontinue, supply, replace or alter pipes (paras 15–18).

The Competition and Service (Utilities) Act 1992 gives effect to a government commitment contained in the Citizen's Charter (HMSO, Cm 1599) to give the Directors General for water, gas, electricity and telecommunications further legal powers to ensure that better services are provided for consumers. For each utility the Act provides for the Directors to make regulations for standards of performance, to collect information on levels of performance and to make it available, to establish procedures for dealing with consumers' complaints and to determine disputes, including those on billing and (where relevant) to prevent disconnections in cases where there is a genuine dispute. This last provision will not apply where disputing the bill is a tactic to avoid payment, *Jones v East Ham Corporation* [1935] 1 KB 367.

By s 38 of the 1992 Act, amending the 1986 Act, the Director General is placed under a duty to exercise his functions 'in a manner which he considers is best calculated to secure effective competition between persons whose business consists of or includes the supply of gas'. The aim is that British Gas runs its gas transmission, distribution and storage business as a separate unit so that it serves British Gas on equal terms with other gas shippers. If agreement cannot be reached, the matter can be referred to the Monopolies and Mergers Commission.

2 Right to lay pipes

In order to supply gas to a person whom they are bound or entitled to supply (or in order to receive a bulk supply), the PGS may break up and open any street or bridge (Sched 4, para 1). The PGS must do as little damage as possible and make compensation for all damage done (ibid). Loss of profit to the business of a person affected by the works is possibly included in the term 'damage', despite *Argyle Motors Ltd v Birkenhead Corporation*

[1975] AC 99; see *Leonidis v Thames Water Authority* (1979) 77 LGR 722. A PGS may also open and break up any sewers, drains or tunnels in or under any street or bridge and lay pipes, conduits and service pipes, and repair, alter or remove them but it cannot erect a structure for housing pressure governors in a street or bridge without the consent (not to be unreasonably withheld) of the highway authority (ibid). A board cannot lay its pipes in private land without the consent of the owner and occupier, but it may enter on private land, after giving not less than seven days' notice in writing to the owner and occupier, to repair, replace or alter any pipe lawfully laid there (ibid). No prior notice is required in a case of emergency but notice must be given as soon as possible after the emergency (ibid).

The laying underground of mains, pipes or other apparatus by the PGS does not need an express planning permission as it falls within the Town and Country Planning General Development Order 1988 (SI No 1813, in force from 5 December 1988) Sched 2, Pt 17, Class F. By the conditions attached by Class F2 prior notice must be given to the responsible planning authority before operations commence.

An authorised officer of a PGS may enter on premises at all reasonable times, on showing his documents of authority, to inspect meters, fittings and works for the supply of gas (Sched 5, para 15). Premises may be entered after 24 hours' notice to the occupier (or to the owner or lessee if the premises are unoccupied) for the removal of meters, pipes and fittings, where the occupier ceases to require a supply or where a PGS is authorised to cut off the supply (ibid, para 16). See the Gas Safety (Rights of Entry) Regulations 1983 (SI No 1575), the Gas Safety (Installation and Use) Regulations 1994 (SI No 1886) and the Gas Appliances (Safety) Regulations 1992 (SI No 711).

A person who installs or alters gas equipment in or on premises must do so in accordance with the safety standards laid down in the Gas Safety (Installation and Use) Regulations 1994 (SI No 1886).

3 Street works

A PGS is subject to the New Roads and Street Works Act 1991 (which replaces the Public Utilities Street Works Act 1950). Schedule 8 of the 1991 Act amends Sched 4 of the Gas Act 1986.

The result is that a PGS, by Sched 4, may place under any street or bridge and from time to time repair, alter or remove, pipes, conduits, service pipes, sewers and other works, and pressure governors, ventilators and other apparatus.

For these purposes it may open or break up any street, bridge, sewer, drain or tunnel (para 1). It may not do this in land not dedicated to public use, unless for the purpose of giving a supply of gas to premises which abut on the street (para 3).

4 Nuisance by a PGS

A PGS shall do as little damage as possible in the exercise of its powers and shall make compensation for damage done in such exercise (Sched 4, para 1(3)). It is not liable for nuisance if it did not cause or adopt the nuisance (*Dunne v North Western Gas Board* [1964] 2 QB 806 (CA)). A PGS is liable criminally if it fails within 12 hours of receiving notice of the escape of gas to prevent it unless it can show that compliance was not reasonably practicable within the time and that it did comply as soon as it was reasonably practicable to do so (Sched 5, para 13).

Where a statutory undertaker causes a nuisance which is attributable to its carrying out of street works under statutory power, the authority is not liable unless it has also been negligent (*Department of Transport v North West Water Authority* [1983] 3 WLR 707 (HL), construing the Public Utilities Street Works Act 1950, s 18(2)).

5 Damage to property of a PGS

A person who intentionally or by culpable negligence injures or allows to be injured any pipes, meter or fittings of a PGS may be prosecuted and liable to a fine not exceeding level 3 on the standard scale (Sched 5, para 10).

A PGS may decline to supply gas to any person who improperly uses it or so deals with it as to interfere with the efficient supply to any other consumer (Sched 5, para 9).

A person will be liable to a PGS for damaging pipes properly laid in streets, by reason of extraordinary traffic such as a very heavy load (*Gas Light & Coke Co v St Mary Abbott's, Kensington, Vestry* (1885) 15 QBD 1: gas pipes under a road were damaged by a heavy steamroller carrying out street repairs—a claim for the damage was successful).

6 Underground storage of gas

The Gas Act 1965 authorises a PGS to store gas in natural porous strata underground provided they have a storage authorisation order from the Secretary of State (1965 Act, s 4). He may at any time impose conditions on the manner of storage if he considers it necessary to do so in the interests of safety (s 16), and a PGS is absolutely liable in civil proceedings for damage caused by gas in underground gas storage or in boreholes connected with underground gas storage or by an escape of gas from storage or boreholes (s 14). Compensation is payable where percolating water is polluted by the underground gas, whether stored or escaped (s 15). In addition to designating an area for storage, the Secretary of State may designate an area (called 'the protective area') within which excavating, mining, quarrying or boring below a prescribed depth is controlled so as not to cause the danger of escapes of gas (s 5). Particulars of the storage area and protective area are registrable as local land charges (s 5(10)). A person who proves that his interest in land is depreciated in value by reason of the making of a storage authorisation order is entitled to compensation equal to the amount of the depreciation (s 7). The compensation is assessed by the Lands Tribunal (s 23) if the parties do not agree it.

The form of the storage authorisation order and the procedure for applying for it are set out in Sched 2 to the Gas Act 1965. By para 1 of Sched 2 a storage authorisation order shall specify by reference to a large-scale map attached to the order the extent and location of the stratum (and the surface perimeter) in which gas may be stored ('the storage area'); it shall state the nature of the gas authorised to be stored, and specify the protective area.

When applying for an authorisation order the applicants must first supply written proposals giving such details as the perimeter of the storage area and protective area, the depth of proposed storage, the nature and volume of gas, the proposed method of injecting and withdrawing gas and particulars of exploratory work done and results obtained (Gas Act 1965, Sched 2, para 3(2)). Notice of the proposals must be published on two successive weeks in the Gazette and local newspapers circulating in the area, saying where the detailed proposals and map may be inspected (para 4(1)). Copies of the notice must be served on every local planning authority, local authority and water authority in the area and on such other body or person as the Secretary of State may direct (para 4(2)). He will then decide whether to allow a formal application or not; he may allow it to proceed with modifications (para 5). The formal application to the Secretary of State will give a specification of the surface works, boreholes and pipes; a large scale map showing the perimeters of the storage area and protective area; sufficient particulars of any surface works; a statement of depth of storage; and particulars of the nature and volume of gas to be stored (para 6(1)). There must be notice by advertisements again in the Gazette and local newspapers on two successive weeks; the notice will state (inter alia) that objections to the Secretary of State must be made not less than 28 days from the date of first publication of the notice (para 7(2)). A copy of the notice must be served on every local planning authority, local authority, National Rivers Authority or Environment Agency as relevant, statutory water undertaker and highway authority in the area affected, on every owner, lessee and occupier (except tenants for a month or less) within the storage area or protective area and on such other persons or bodies as the Secretary of State may direct (para 7(3), as amended by the Gas Act 1986). If an objection is made which is not trivial or frivolous and does not merely relate to compensation, he must hold a public local enquiry (para 8). The procedure is governed by the Gas (Underground Storage) (Inquiries Procedure) Rules 1966 (SI No 1375). If the order is made, the applicants must publish in the Gazette and local newspapers a notice to that effect and must serve the notice on every person who was entitled to be notified of the application to the Secretary of State (para 10(6), (7)). A copy of the order and map must be lodged with each local authority (para 10(7)).

A PGS may obtain by compulsory purchase the right to store gas in an underground gas storage (Gas Act 1965, s 12(1)). Liquified natural gas is stored in six major installations and in five salt cavities near Hornsea (British Gas Annual Report 1988, p 8). The Secretary of State may also authorise a PGS under para 1 of Sched 3 to the 1986 Act to purchase compulsorily any land which is in a storage area or protective area which is the site of any well, borehole or shaft, in order to use the well, borehole or shaft in connection with the underground gas storage or (where it goes below the depth at which the gas is stored) to block it up or stop anyone else from using it (1965 Act, s 13(1)). A right of way for access to land on which there is, or is to be made, a well, borehole or shaft may be compulsorily granted also, and the grant of this will carry with it any necessary ancillary rights, such as to construct and maintain gates, stiles and bridges along the way (s 13(3)).

7 Environmental impact

By the Electricity and Pipe-Line Works (Assessment of Environmental Effects) Regulations 1990 (SI No 442), on any application for a pipe-line authorisation or diversion for a pipe-line which is intended to carry oil or gas, an environmental statement must be supplied to the Secretary of State. He will send copies to interested parties and allow representations to be made and considered. The statement must show the likely significant effects, direct and indirect, of the development on human beings, flora, fauna, soil, water, air, climate and the cultural heritage. It must state the measures proposed to be taken to avoid, reduce or remedy the effects. In 1992 the Department of Trade and Industry issued guidelines for the environmental assessment of cross-country pipe-lines.

8 Compulsory purchase and compensation

A PGS may be authorised by the Secretary of State to purchase compulsorily any land (including any right over land, and to create and acquire new rights) which is required for or in connection with the exercise and performance of its functions (s 9(3), Sched 3, para 1). The procedure laid down in the Acquisition of Land Act 1981, Sched 1, and the Compulsory Purchase Act 1965, applies (Sched 2, paras 4, 5). Notices must be served on the owners and occupiers and advertisements made. They can object and the Secretary of State may then hold a public enquiry. Compensation is payable, assessed by the Lands Tribunal if agreement cannot otherwise be reached, at an open market value under the Land Compensation Act 1961, s 5. Compensation is also payable for injurious affection, severance or disturbance, just as in the case of the laying of sewers, already discussed. In *Wells-Kendrew v British Gas Corporation* (1974) 229 EG 272, the following sums were paid: 12½p per linear yard for the laying of an 18-inch natural gas pipe for 211 yards in woodland in a 20-foot wide strip; 25p per linear yard for the pipe-line for a 20-foot wide strip 541 yards long in pasture land. The total payment was £162.50. In *Vaynor Developments v Wales Gas Board* [1977] CLY 332 the claimants bought land with planning permission for 15 houses, subject to

the Water Board's rights over a 40 foot wide strip. Shortly after-
wards the Board extended rights to a 320 foot strip. Because of
this the claimants abandoned negotiations with builders for a
development of 69 houses for which planning permission was
virtually assured. The claimants asked for £51,000 on the basis
that they had nearly reached agreement for the development; the
Board offered £11,500 on a sale-price basis. The sum of £27,000
was awarded on a 'ripe for development' basis but the higher
claim was discounted for uncertainty, risk and deferment. Compensation may need to be negotiated for such things as the disturbance and checking of trees when a main is laid under or near to
them, and for minerals which must remain in the ground unworked
because of the danger that working would cause subsidence to the
mains.

In *Collins v Thames Water Utilities Ltd* (1994) 9449 EG 116
(Lands Tribunal) a sewer was laid at a depth of 700mm across the
bottom of the garden of a private house, with a protected area of
6m, amounting to some 36 per cent of the garden. Previously the
house was served by a septic tank but was now connected to
the new sewer (which served 420 houses). Compensation was
awarded of £415 for entry, disturbance and claimants' time but
nothing was awarded for injurious affection to the property as
the enhancement in utility and value meant that there was no
detrimental effect, even though there was a right of future entry
and a protected area.

In *Whelan v British Gas* [1993] 2 EGLR 243, the plaintiff owned
agricultural land through which gas pipe-lines had been laid in
1971 under a deed of grant of easements which forbade the deposit
of any matter over the pipe-lines. In 1980 British Gas laid another
two adjacent pipe-lines under compulsory powers. As part of the
claim for severance and injurious affection W claimed that he had
lost the development rights of tipping given by the Town and
Country Planning General Development Order 1977 (SI No 289),
Sched 1, Class VI. He failed; because of the terms of the deed of
1971 no such rights existed over the pipe-lines.

Under a national agreement between the Country Landowners'
Association, the National Farmers' Union and the Gas Industry,
rates of compensation for such things as the grant of an easement
for a gas main, disturbance payments, loss of development value,
and the mining of minerals, have been agreed. The rate will vary
according to the value per acre of the land affected and the width
of the strip affected. Compensation is based on 80 per cent of the

land value. There is a minimum payment of £1.50 per yard affecting smaller pipes on land of lower value, except moorland. The
occupier's payment is: 18 inches and smaller, £1.25 per yard; 24
inches and 30 inches diameter pipes, £1.80 per yard; 36 inches,
42 inches and 48 inches pipes, £2.05 per yard.

It is understood from the Country Landowners' Association
that for gas pipe-lines the CLA and the NFU try to negotiate at
the start of a gaslines project for a capital sum relating to the whole
length of the pipe-line, though individual owners may negotiate for
themselves if they wish over such land as, for example, market
gardens, organic farms and development land. The standard deed
of grant negotiated by the CLA and the NFU makes the pipe-
line operator responsible for any drainage problems which arise
as a result of the pipe-line, in perpetuity, and also permits further
compensation to be paid as and when development is frustrated
because of the pipe.

9 Gas Act 1995

The Gas Act 1995 will, when it takes full effect in 1998, intro-
duce a licensing framework which will allow gas to be supplied
under licence granted by the Director General of Gas Supply
('the Director') so as to allow full competition. There has been
competition in supply to industrial and commercial markets from
1987, under the Gas Act 1986; the 1995 Act enables small businesses using less than 2,500 therms annually, as well as householders, to have a competitive gas supply, according to the
explanatory memorandum issued with the Bill.

Licensing

Section 3(1) amends the 1986 Act by prohibiting the conveyance
of gas to premises or to a pipe-line system operated by a public
gas transporter; or the supply to premises of gas which has been
conveyed to them through pipes; or arrangements with a public
gas transporter for gas to be introduced into or taken out of a
pipe-line system operated by that transporter, without a licence.
By ss 5 and 6 licences are needed by public gas transporters (who
operate the pipe-line system through which the gas is delivered),
gas shippers (who arrange with public gas transporters for gas in
appropriate amounts to be moved through the pipe-line system)
and gas suppliers (who sell piped gas to consumers). Licences are

granted by the Director, by the procedures mentioned in ss 5–7 and under standard conditions mentioned in s 8, subject to modification as the Director 'considers requisite to meet the circumstances of the particular case', s 8(2). All these changes are effected by amendments to the 1986 Act.

The gas code

Section 9 and Sched 2 revise the 'gas supply code' (1986 Act, s 15 and Sched 5) to take account of the new framework. It is renamed the 'gas code'.

Schedule 2 deals with such matters as: the offences of injuring a gas fitting or service pipe or interfering with the gas meter intentionally or by culpable negligence (reg 8(1)), restoring the supply without consent (reg 9(1)), failing to notify connection or disconnection of a service pipe (reg 10(1)), powers of a public gas transporter to enter premises on reasonable suspicion of a gas escape, or to prevent an escape, or on discontinuance of a supply, or to replace, repair or alter pipes (on reasonable notice), regs 15–17, 19 and 20.

Duty to supply and standards of quality

By Sched 3, reg 3, it shall be the duty of a public gas transporter to develop and maintain an efficient and economical pipe-line system for the conveyance of gas; and so far as it is economical to do so, to comply with any reasonable request to connect a person to the system and to convey gas to his premises; undue preference or undue discrimination in the connection or terms of supply shall be avoided.

By reg 4, the duty to connect contained in s 10 of the 1986 Act is replaced by a duty under this regulation. Premises in an authorised area of a public gas transporter which are within 23 metres from a relevant main, or are connected to the main, or could be so connected by a service pipe supplied and laid by the owner of the premises, are to be connected (where necessary) and supplied thereafter. No connection can be required by a person whose need for a supply is likely to exceed 75,000 therms in any period of 12 months (new s 10(5) of the 1986 Act).

Schedule 3, reg 12 supplies a new s 16 to the 1986 Act. It says that the Director shall, after consultation with public gas suppliers, prescribe standards of pressure and purity for all transporters and may, after consultation, prescribe other standards with regard to properties, condition and composition of gas.

By Sched 3, reg 16, which introduces a substituted s 19 to the 1986 Act, other persons may be authorised by the Director to use the pipe-line systems of a public gas transporter for the transport of gas of a specified kind or of a kind similar to that which the system is designed to convey. If the Director is satisfied that giving directions under s 19 would not prejudice the conveyance in the pipe-line of the quantities of gas which the public gas transporter would reasonably expect to convey, he may permit its use by the transporter on specified terms, s 19(3), (4).

Chapter 12

Street Works

1 Highway authorities

Under s 1(2) (as amended) of the Highways Act 1980 ('HA') each county council or metropolitan district council is the highway authority outside Greater London for highways which are not trunk roads or other special roads. For trunk or special roads the highway authority is the Secretary of State for the Environment (HA, s 1(1) as amended by the New Roads and Street Works Act 1991 ('NRSWA'), s 21) though he may enter into an agreement for the county council to exercise some of his functions (and they, with his consent, may agree for a district council to exercise). In London the highway authority is the metropolitan district council (it was formerly the Greater London Council) for metropolitan roads and the appropriate non-metropolitan council for highways (s 1(3)). Outside London the district council may maintain public highways (s 42(1)). The Greater London Council and the metropolitan county councils were abolished from 1 April 1986 by the Local Government Act 1985, s 1.

2 The making up of private streets

The private street works code is contained in HA, ss 205–218. Where a street works authority considers that any private street within its area is not sewered, levelled, paved, metalled, flagged, channelled, made good and lighted to its satisfaction it may resolve to carry out street works and, subject to the private street works code, the expenses so incurred shall be apportioned between the premises fronting the street (HA, s 205(1)). By s 203(1) 'the private street works code' means ss 205–218.

By HA, s 329(1) and NRSWA, s 48(1) the term 'street' includes

148

any highway, road, lane, footpath, square, court, alley, or passage whether a thoroughfare or not, and any part of a street. By s 328(1) 'highway' means the whole or part of a highway, other than a ferry or waterway, except where the context otherwise requires.

By HA, s 206 a street works authority may include in street works to be executed any works which the authority thinks necessary for bringing the street, as regards sewerage, drainage, level, or other matters, into conformity with other streets, including the provision of separate sewers for the reception of sewage and of surface water respectively. Under the 1980 Code the proper officer of the road authority prepares specifications, makes an estimate of probable cost and a provisional apportionment of cost 'between the premises liable to be charged with them' (s 205(3)), that is, those 'fronting the street' (s 205(1)). By s 203(3) 'fronting' includes 'adjoining'. By s 207(3) the authority may include in the apportionment premises which do not front the street but have access to it through a court, passage or otherwise if they will in the authority's view be benefited by the works; the contribution will be fixed according to the degree of benefit to be derived by the premises. The apportionment upon premises liable to be charged is in general made 'according to the frontage of the respective premises' (s 207(1)). A person can be a frontager even if his premises are separated from the street by, for example, a strip of waste land (*Warwickshire County Council v Adkins* (1967) 112 SJ 135). The owner of a first floor maisonette was held not to be a frontager in *Buckinghamshire County Council v Trigg* [1963] 1 WLR 155.

After the provisional apportionment has been made the authority resolves to adopt the specifications and public advertisement of the scheme is made (s 205(5)). Copies are served on the owners affected and they may object within one month of publication (s 208(1)). Objections are heard by the magistrates' court (s 209(1)), which may quash in whole or in part or may amend the resolution of approval, specification, plans, sections, estimate and provisional apportionment or any of them (s 209(2)). After the scheme has been approved and objections have been dealt with, the work is carried out by or for the highway authority and the cost is recoverable from the owners for the time being of the premises (s 212(1)), after a final apportionment has been made under s 211 and notice has been served on the owners (ibid).

If the owners of property accounting for more than one-half of the frontage of a made up street (or part not less than 100 yards in length) request it, the highway authority must declare the street to be repairable at the public expense, provided that security has been given under s 219 and not refunded or released (s 229).

By s 37 a highway may become repairable at the public expense by dedication by any person, if the authority does not decline to accept it. By s 38 a highway authority may adopt a highway by agreement with a person and thereupon the liability of that person to maintain will be extinguished. By s 41(1) if a highway is maintainable at the public expense the highway authority is under a duty to maintain the highway.

By s 69(1) of the Housing Act 1988, when any street works have been executed in a private street in an area designated as the area of a housing action trust, the trust may serve a notice on the street works authority requiring it to declare the street a highway maintainable at the public expense. The highway authority may within two months of the service of the notice appeal to the Secretary of State on grounds relating to its construction, design, layout or maintenance (s 69(2)). The Secretary may determine the appeal and may impose conditions on the trust, on compliance with which the notice will take effect (s 69(3), (4)).

3 The making of roads by developers

The system of payment for work to be done is known as 'the advance payments code' and by HA, s 203(1) the phrase means ss 219–225.

By s 219(1), where it is proposed to erect a building for which plans are required to be lodged with the local authority for building regulations permission and the building will front onto a private street for which the street works authority will have power under the relevant street works code to require works to be executed or to execute works, no work shall be done to erect the building unless a sufficient sum for the cost of the street works has been paid to the authority or has been secured to the satisfaction of the authority. Certain exceptions, such as where the street is not joined, or likely to be joined for a reasonable time, to the public highway, are given in s 219(4). The street works authority then calculates what sum would be recoverable if the authority itself carried out such work as the authority would require before declaring the street to be one maintainable at the public expense (s 220(3)). Within six weeks of passing the developer's plans the authority serves notice on him requiring the payment or the securing of the sum specified in the notice (s 220(1)). He can then deposit the sum with the authority or, much more usually, enter into an agreement with the authority under s 38. Under such an agreement the developer agrees to construct the roads within a stated time to the standard laid down by the authority and the authority in turn agrees to maintain the works when they have been completed and take them over in a stated time, for mainten-ance at the public expense. The s 38 agreement is almost invariably supported by a bond, in which an insurance company, bank or similar institution guarantees due performance by providing the money for completion of the works if the developer defaults. The respective obligations of those parties were discussed in *National Employers' Mutual General Insurance Association v Herne Bay District Council* (1972) 70 LGR 542. It was held in *Overseas Investment Services Ltd v Simcobuild Construction Ltd* (1993) *The Times*, 2 November; [1993] CLYB 544 that a s 38 agreement to dedicate land as a public highway created an overriding interest under s 70(1)(*a*) of the Land Registration Act 1925 which bound a purchaser of a legal or equitable estate in the land.

The authority which enters into s 38 agreements differs with the area and the nature of the road. By s 1, for example, the Minister is the highway authority for trunk roads but by s 6 he may delegate his functions to a county council, a metropolitan district council or a London borough council; outside the former GLC area the county council is the highway authority for all except trunk roads but by s 42 the non-metropolitan district council may undertake maintenance of any eligible highway in the district and many s 38 agreements are made by the non-metropolitan district council.

4 Street works by statutory bodies

The New Roads and Street Works Act 1991, Pt III, replaces the code which, under the Public Utilities Street Works Act 1950, regulated statutory undertakers in such matters as breaking up streets in order to carry out operations on sewers, drains and tunnels under roads, and laying apparatus there. The basic require-ment of the NRSWA is that for anyone other than the 'street authority' to place apparatus in a street or to break or open a street, sewer, drain or tunnel under it or to tunnel or bore under a street for the purpose of placing, repairing, altering or removing apparatus, a licence from the street authority is required (s 50 and Sched 3).

The licence will permit the works without the need for a licence from any other authority, such as a sewer or bridge authority, s 50(1). The 'street authority' is the highway authority if the street is a maintainable one, or otherwise it refers to the street managers, s 49(1). By s 48(1) a 'street' means the whole or any part of any highway, road, lane, footway, alley or passage, square or court, any land laid out as a way whether formed or not and a bridge or tunnel where a street passes over or through it, s 48(1). Emergency works, where the works are required to avoid danger to persons or property, need no licence, s 52(1).

The street authority is required to keep a register of street works, open for public inspection s 53(1). There is a general duty on the street authority to co-ordinate works in the interests of safety and to minimise inconvenience to users of the street, s 59(1). The Secretary of State may issue codes of practice giving practical guidance, s 59(3).

By ss 55(1) and 89(2), an undertaker who proposes to execute street works involving breaking up or opening up any street, or sewer, drain or tunnel under it, or tunnelling or boring under it, shall give not less than seven days notice to the street authority and to any other relevant authority whose apparatus is likely to be affected by the work. If it appears to the street authority that the works are likely to cause serious disruption to traffic and that this could be lessened, they may give directions as to time of working, s 56(1). If substantial road works are to be carried out the authority may direct that further street works are to be restricted for the next twelve months, s 58(1).

The undertaker must take safety measures with particular regard to the needs of persons with a disability, s 65(1). They must avoid unnecessary delay or obstruction and shall, on pain of conviction, carry out the works with all reasonable dispatch, s 66(1). Reinstatement must begin as soon as any part of the work is completed and be fully completed with all reasonable dispatch, s 70(1). Temporary and permanent reinstatement must be carried out to standards prescribed by the Secretary of State, s 71(1). If the reinstatement does not accord with the standards, the street authority may carry out the necessary works and recover the costs from the undertaker, s 72(3). The Street Works (Reinstatement) Regulations 1992 (SI No 1689) as amended, apply.

Ministerial Circulars concerning street works can be found in the *Encyclopaedia of Highway Law* (Sweet & Maxwell) vols 3 and 4. Circular 28/93 explains the street works provisions of NRSWA 1991, vol 4, para 6–1469.

Drainage onto the highway

A local authority or highway authority may serve notice on the occupier of premises adjoining a highway requiring him within 28 days to construct such channels, gutters or downpipes as will prevent water falling from his roof or any other part of the premises onto people using the highway and as will prevent (so far as reasonably practicable) surface water from flowing onto or over the footway (HA, s 163(1)).

Bridging a highway

The highway authority may grant a person a licence to construct a bridge over a highway on such terms and conditions as it thinks fit. It cannot charge him for the licence, except for legal or other expenses, but he must remove the bridge when the authority requires him to do so, if the authority needs to improve the highway (HA, s 176).

The bridge authority must be consulted before the start of street works which will affect its structure (NRSWA, s 88(3)).

Building over a highway

By HA, s 177(1) except in the exercise of statutory powers no building may be constructed over any part of a highway maintainable at the public expense, without a licence from the highway authority; and no building constructed or altered under such a licence shall be used otherwise than in accordance with the terms and conditions of the licence.

Pipes over highway

No person may without the consent of the highway authority (which it may grant on such reasonable terms and conditions as it thinks fit) fix or place any overhead beam, rail, pipe, cable, wire or other similar apparatus over, along or across a highway (HA, s 178(1)). Appeal on a refusal or as to the reasonableness of conditions is to a magistrates' court (s 178(2)). Section 178 does not apply to any works or apparatus of statutory undertakers, including the Civil Aviation Authority, the Post Office and the operator of any telecommunications code system (Telecommunications Act 1984, s 109 and Sched 4).

Vaults and cellars under highway

No one may construct any part of a building or a vault, arch or cellar under a carriageway of a street without the consent of the appropriate authority (HA, s 179(1)), nor make an opening in a footway as an entrance to a vault or cellar (s 180(1)). Every vault, arch and cellar under a street and every opening from the street into such works shall be kept in good condition and repair by the owner or occupier (s 180(6)). A breach of s 180(6) does not of itself give rise to a civil action; there must be negligence or nuisance by the person responsible for repair before an action will lie. In *Scott v Green & Sons* [1969] 1 WLR 301 (CA) a builder's lorry cracked a flagstone over the defendants' cellar, unknown to the defendants. Minutes later the plaintiff fell into the cellar and was injured. The defendants were held not liable. But where a person was injured because her leg went through a defective grating of which the occupier knew, he was liable in nuisance, *MacFarlane v Gwalter* [1958] 1 All ER 181.

Chapter 13

Pipe-lines

1 Pipe-lines Act 1962

The purposes of the Act are to place the control of cross-country pipe-lines in the hands of the Secretary of State for the Environment to be exercised in the public interest; to enable those wishing to construct pipe-lines to do so without a private Act; to enable the Secretary of State to regulate safely the construction, operation and maintenance of pipe-lines; and to make the pipe-lines rateable.

All references in this chapter are to the Pipe-lines Act 1962 unless otherwise stated.

Definition and scope

Section 65 defines a pipe-line within the Act as a pipe or system of pipes (with any apparatus and associated works) for the conveyance of anything other than air, water, water vapour or steam. The term does not include a drain or sewer, pipes for heating, cooling or domestic purposes, pipes used in building or engineering operations, pipes within the boundaries of an agricultural unit and designed for use for agriculture (defined in s 66), pipes in premises used for education or research, or a pneumatic dispatch-tube. Pipes of a public gas supplier, the electricity boards, PowerGen, National Power and the United Kingdom Atomic Energy Authority are excluded (s 58). Much of the Act does not apply to pipe-lines of railway undertakers, dock pipe-lines or government pipe-lines (ss 59, 61, 62), or to pipe-lines in factories, mines, quarry premises or petroleum depots (s 60). Cement and chalk slurry, oxygen, brine and ethylene gas are now being piped. There is an oil pipe-line 254 miles long linking the Thames and

Mersey estuaries ((1969) *The Times*, 20 March), and a natural gas pipe-line running from Italy to the USSR ((1978) *The Times*, 23 March). A feasibility study for a gas pipe-line from Iran to India across the Arabian Sea was announced in 1995 ((1995) *The Times*, 18 January).

Control of construction

Sections 1 and 2 state that a cross country pipe-line (one more than ten miles long: s 66) may not be constructed without the consent of the Secretary of State by means of a pipe-line construction authorisation, and that a local pipe-line (one not exceeding ten miles in length: s 66) may not be constructed unless a notice of intention to construct has been served on the Secretary of State not less than 16 weeks before construction begins.

Distances and dimensions given in this chapter are as stated in the Act but have now been converted by the Pipe-lines (Metrication) Regulations 1992 (SI No 449).

Part I of Sched 1 sets out the particulars to be given on application for pipe-line construction authorisation, such as three copies of a map of the proposed route, particulars of any consents needed and obtained and a statement of what will be conveyed in the pipe-line (para 1). Notice of the application to the Secretary of State must be published in the *London Gazette* and be given in any other manner that he may direct, and must indicate where the map can be inspected and how objections can be lodged. Notice must also be served on the local planning authorities through whose area the pipe will go and on any other person that the Secretary of State may specify (para 3). He must hold a public enquiry if a local planning authority objects to the proposals; in the case of any other objector he may either hold a public enquiry or allow the objector to appear before a person appointed by him for the purpose; he may hold a public enquiry even though no local planning authority has objected (para 4).

If the Secretary of State grants an authorisation, construction work must be substantially begun within 12 months of the grant, but he may grant an extension of time (s 1(4)).

By the Pipe-lines (Limits of Deviation) Regulations 1962 (SI No 2845), as amended by the Pipe-lines (Metrication) Regulations 1992 (SI No 449) from 1 January 1995, a deviation of not more than 100 feet laterally from the route shown on the deposited map is permitted.

Where notice is given to the Secretary of State of intention to construct a local pipe-line the notice must give similar particulars to those listed in the case of a cross-country pipe-line (and the applicant must send a copy of the plan to the local authority: s 35(2)), and again the work, if permitted, must be substantially begun within 12 months of his consent (s 2). There is no provision for advertisement, objection or public enquiry in this case, except that the Secretary of State may by statutory instrument direct that the procedure of s 1 shall apply to applications for the construction of local pipe-lines of the class specified in the order (s 6). By a new s 6A (added by s 25 of the Petroleum Act 1987) a pipe-line construction authorisation shall not allow a modified route for a pipe unless at least 28 days notice has been given to the local planning authority and any person specified by the Minister. If there are objections a public enquiry must be held. If an addition to a pipe-line already less than ten miles long would make it exceed ten miles, or the joining of two or more would make them in total exceed ten miles in length, then the procedure of s 1 for cross country pipe-lines must be followed (s 7).

The procedure for an application to lay must be followed where there is a wish to divert a cross-country or local pipe-line (s 3). Where the Secretary of State grants authority to lay or divert, he may at the same time grant the appropriate planning permission (s 5(1)). The execution of works for inspecting, maintaining, adjusting, repairing, altering or renewing a pipe-line (including breaking open any street or other land) does not constitute 'development' and so does not require planning permission (s 5(2)). Emergency works of construction or diversion may be done without the Secretary of State's prior permission provided permission is obtained as soon as reasonably practicable (s 8).

A person to whom a pipe-line construction or diversion authorisation is granted must forthwith after the grant deposit with each local authority through whose area the pipe is to run a copy of so much of the plan submitted with the application to the Secretary of State as shows the part of the route that lies within that area (s 35(1)). These plans must be open to inspection free of charge at all reasonable hours at the local authority's offices (s 35(5)).

Environmental assessment

By the Electricity and Pipe-line Works (Assessment of Environmental Effects) Regulations 1990 (SI No 442), on any application for a pipe-line authorisation or diversion for a pipe-line which is intended to carry oil or gas, an environmental statement must be supplied to the Secretary of State. He will send copies to interested parties and allow representations to be made and considered. The statement must show the likely significant effects, direct and indirect, of the development on human beings, flora, fauna, soil, water, air, climate and the cultural heritage. It must state the measures proposed to be taken to avoid, reduce or remedy the effects. In 1992 the Department of Trade and Industry issued guidelines for the environmental assessment of cross-country pipe-lines (see also *Guidance Notes for Applications and Notifications for Onshore Pipelines* (HMSO 1993)).

By s 5 of the 1962 Act, the Secretary of State, upon granting a pipe-line construction or diversion authorisation, or serving notice requiring removal of works, may direct that planning permission for the work is deemed to be granted under the (current) Town and Country Planning Act 1990, Pt III, subject to such conditions as to the environmental matters mentioned above as may be specified in his direction.

Pipe-lines in streets

Pipe-lines may be laid in a street which is a maintainable high-way with the consent of the highway authority, in a street which is prospectively a maintainable highway with the consent of the highway authority and the street managers, and in any other street with the consent of the street managers (s 15(1), (10)). The pipe-line owner may open and break up the street to lay, inspect, maintain, adjust, repair, alter, renew or change the position of a pipe-line (s 15(1)). The consent of the appropriate authority may be given on reasonable conditions but must not be unreasonably withheld (s 15(3), (4)). Where the pipe-line is to be placed along a line crossing the street, consent may not be refused unless there are special reasons (s 15(2)). The Secretary of State will determine any disputes as to consents and conditions on the placing in a street of a pipe-line (s 15(6)). Similar disputes as to the placing of a pipe-line along a line crossing the street go to an arbitrator (s 15(7)). The New Roads and Street Works Act 1991 Pt III (replacing the Public Utilities Street Works Act 1950) applies where pipe-lines are to be laid in streets. Part III substitutes a new s 16 for ss 16 and 17 of the 1962 Act in relation to plans, sections and arbitrations in connection with street works.

Safety of pipe-lines

The Health and Safety Executive may by notice to the pipe-line constructor specify in respect of a pipe-line or any part of it the manner of construction, the materials and components to be used and the depth at which the pipe is to be (s 20). A pipe-line owner may be prohibited from using any pipe-line which does not comply with the notice (s 22). The Health and Safety Executive may at any time by notice served on the owner impose such requirements as the Executive thinks fit in the interests of safety for the examination, repair, maintenance, adjustment and testing of the line and the inspection of the route of the line (s 23(1)). The Secretary of State may order, by notice, the owner to carry out works specified in the notice to make an abandoned or disused pipe-line safe (s 25). A pipe-line may not be used for the conveyance of a different class of thing from that originally authorised without the owner giving at least three weeks' notice of intention to the Health and Safety Executive before making the change (s 26).

With the object of preventing free access to a pipe-line from being obstructed, ss 27 and 31 enact that, if a person erects a building or structure so that any part of it is less than ten feet from a point on the surface vertically above the pipe, or if a person deposits any earth, refuse, spoil or other materials within the same distance, the Secretary of State may by notice order him to demolish the building or carry out other work to protect the pipe, or, in the case of the deposit of earth, etc, he may remove it at the expense of the person who deposited it. The Secretary of State may serve on the owner of the building notice of the time (not being less than 21 days from the date of service of the notice) and place at which the question of ordering demolition will be considered and the owners of the building and the pipe-line are entitled to be heard when the question is considered (s 27(2)).

Compulsory acquisition

The Secretary of State may authorise the compulsory purchase of land by a person proposing to lay a pipe-line (s 11(1)), or may authorise the placing of a pipe-line in land by means of a compulsory rights order (s 12(1)). Where compulsory purchase is applied for to the Secretary of State, the applicant must follow the procedure of Sched 2, Pt I. The applicant lodges with the Secretary of State three copies of a large scale map (not less than six inches to the mile), showing the land proposed to be acquired (para 1 (*b*)). The Secretary of State may either reject the application or order that it be allowed to proceed (para 2). If he allows it to proceed there must be advertisements on two successive weeks in one or more local newspapers stating that the application has been made, and saying where the map has been lodged and where objection can be made: a notice of the application must also be served on every owner, lessee and occupier (except tenants for a month or less) giving at least 28 days in which to object to the Secretary of State (para 3). The form of the notice is prescribed in the Pipe-lines (Notices) Regulations 1963 (SI No 151). Where an owner, lessee or occupier objects the Secretary of State may either hold a public enquiry or allow the objector and applicant an opportunity of appearing before a person appointed by him (para 4). The procedure is governed by the Pipe-lines (Inquiries Procedure) Rules 1967 (SI No 1769), operative from 1 January 1968. Where the Secretary of State refuses to grant a compulsory purchase order he must give the applicant a written statement of his reasons for refusing (para 5). Where the order is granted the applicant must publish the fact in one or more local newspapers, describing the land and saying where a copy order and map may be inspected, and must serve a similar notice on each owner, lessee and occupier of land comprised in the order (para 7(2)). Appeal to the High Court within six weeks of the order becoming operative is possible on the grounds only that the order made was not authorised by the Act or that any requirement or regulation of the Act has not been complied with (para 9(1)).

The same procedure, with the appropriate modifications set out in Sched 2, Pt II, applies to applications for compulsory rights orders. Where the Secretary of State grants such an order he may attach such conditions as he thinks fit concerning (inter alia) the manner, method or timing of the carrying out of the works authorised (s 13(1)). Schedule 4 sets out the ancillary rights which may be conferred by a compulsory rights order, such as a right of access to the pipe by the pipe owner, with or without vehicles, and to deposit on the land temporarily materials brought by such vehicles and required in connection with the pipe; a right to place and renew markers to indicate its position; a right to erect stiles, gates, bridges or culverts to facilitate access to the pipe; and a right to construct works named in the order to facilitate maintenance, inspection or protection from damage.

Compensation

By the Compulsory Purchase Act 1965, where an order for compulsory acquisition is made, a person cannot be made to sell part only of a house, building or manufactory, or of a park or garden belonging to a house, if he is willing to sell the whole, unless the part of the premises can be taken without material detriment to the rest, or the part of the land can be taken without seriously affecting the amenity or convenience of the house (1965 Act, s 8(1)); if a part only is taken, compensation shall be payable for loss caused by severance (1965 Act, s 7). Account shall not be taken of works which in the view of the Lands Tribunal were done on the land with a view to obtaining compensation or increased compensation (1962 Act, Sched 3, para 3).

Where an order for compulsory rights acquisition is made and a person entitled to an interest in the land affected proves that the value of his interest is depreciated by reason of the making of the order, he shall be entitled to compensation equal to the amount of the depreciation (1962 Act, s 14(1)). There is also a right to compensation for damage to, or disturbance in the enjoyment of, any land or chattels by reason of the exercise of any rights conferred by a compulsory rights order (s 14(2)). An example would be damage to crops caused by the pipe-line owner exercising his right of access to the pipe for inspection or maintenance conferred in Sched 4.

Undertakings to safeguard landowners

A series of safeguards has been agreed by the Country Landowners' Association and the National Farmers' Union with certain pipeline promoters. The safeguards are listed in a publication of the Country Landowners' Association entitled *Wayleaves and Easements* (1989) obtainable from the Association, 16 Belgrave Square, London, SW1.

The safeguards cover such items as the depth of the pipe-line (not less than three feet, 900mm underground), trial borings, notice of entry (not less than one month), restoration of the land and hedges, ditches, land drains and watercourses, avoidance of pollution of water supplies or interference with water supplies and drains, insurance of the pipe-line by the company laying it, width of working strip during construction (normally 40 feet only), cathodic protection of buildings, compensation for loss of future development rights, protection of fishing and sporting rights, erection by the company of stock proof fences to keep out stock whilst the pipe is laid, notice of intended inspection and carrying out of works (the right to inspect and carry out works to be suspended if the area is infected because of foot and mouth disease, fowl pest, swine fever or other notifiable disease), and provisions for rendering the pipe-line and ancillary works harmless on abandonment.

An agreement should provide that it is the responsibility of the pipe-layer to lift it and make good the land when use of the pipe has ceased. If this is not done and the pipe deteriorates, pollution of the land may result. The landowner might then be held liable, on the basis of 'polluter pays'.

2 Government oil pipe-lines

Permanent power to maintain

The Requisitioned Land and War Works Act 1948 ('1948 Act') made permanent certain government war works which were originally authorised only temporarily. Any government oil pipe-line may continue to be used provided that the original rights to maintain and use have been registered as local land charges or endorsed on the title deeds of the land affected by it (1948 Act, s 14). A government oil pipe-line is defined in s 12 as any government war works being the whole or part of a main or pipe installed for the transmission of petroleum.

Where there is a right to retain and use a pipe-line, there is ancillary to it the right to remove or replace the pipe-line and by agreement to divert it (s 12). Where an oil pipe-line or accessory works are to be abandoned, notice of the intention to abandon must be given by the Secretary of State for the Environment to every owner and occupier (s 15). The Secretary of State must thereupon remove all sections of the pipe above ground and restore the land to its former level unless otherwise agreed with the owner and occupier (ibid), or unless in the Secretary of State's view it is not reasonably practicable to do this (Government Oil Pipe-Lines Regulations 1959 (SI No 715, reg 4). The pipe-lines and other works if not abandoned must be kept in good repair and persons who are caused injury or loss by a failure to repair must be compensated (1948 Act, s 15).

Compulsory acquisition

The Secretary of State may acquire any land required for constructing oil installations essential to defence; any land containing oil installations which were government war works immediately before 7 July 1948; and any easement necessary for the full enjoyment of land on which an installation is or is to be made (Land Powers (Defence) Act 1958, s 13) ('1958 Act'). Where the land cannot be obtained by agreement the Secretary of State has compulsory powers and he can take possession of the land immediately after giving notice to treat to the owner and occupier, subject to giving not less than fourteen days' notice and to paying compensation 1958 (1958 Act, Sched 2).

Wayleave orders

Oil pipe-lines may be laid under wayleave orders made by certain ministries where the pipe-line is needed for defence purposes (1958 Act, s 14). The right to lay comprises also the right to maintain, replace and remove (s 25). The order is registrable as a local land charge and will not bind a purchaser of a legal estate for money or money's worth in land affected if it is not registered (s 17). Compensation is payable for damage or depreciation to the value of land caused by the laying of the pipe-line (s 18). The ministry making the wayleave order may be ordered by Treasury regulations to keep the pipe-lines in good repair, and indemnify for loss or damage caused if it fails to do so (s 15). Regulations have been made under ss 15 and 18 as to repair and compensation for depreciation in the value of land because of the wayleave order: Government Oil Pipe-Lines (No 2) Regulations 1959 (SI No 724).

Protection

Where an oil pipe-line or accessory works are made or proposed under the various powers outlined above, the construction of buildings, roads or hard standing for vehicles and the excavation or deposit of earth, refuse or spoil may not take place within ten feet of the surface of the land immediately above the pipe-line or works without the consent of the Secretary of State (1958 Act, s 16). Where a wayleave order is made, mining under or near the pipe-line can be prevented subject to the payment of compensation for the minerals forbidden to be mined (s 15).

3 Petroleum and submarine pipe-lines

The Petroleum and Submarine Pipe-Lines Act 1975 set up a body corporate, the British National Oil Corporation (s 1), and gave it the power (among other things) to search for and get petroleum existing in its natural condition in strata in any part of the world, to move, store and treat petroleum and anything derived from it and to buy, sell and otherwise deal in petroleum and anything derived from it (s 2(1)). These powers included a power to provide and operate pipe-lines, tanker ships and refineries in connection with petroleum (s 2(2)(a)). By the Oil and Pipe-lines Act 1985 the British National Oil Corporation was dissolved and its property rights and liabilities were vested in the Oil and Pipelines Agency (ss 1–3). The 1985 Act repealed ss 1–19 inclusive of the 1975 Act.

Construction

By s 20(1) of the 1975 Act a pipe-line may not be constructed or used in, over or under any 'controlled waters' without an authorisation in writing from the Secretary of State. 'Controlled waters' means the territorial sea adjacent to the United Kingdom and the sea in any designated area within the meaning of the Continental Shelf Act 1964, and 'controlled pipe-line' means any pipe-line in, under or over controlled waters (s 20(2)). 'Pipe-line' means in Pt III of the Act (ss 20–33) a pipe or system of pipes (excluding a drain or sewer) for the conveyance of anything, together with any apparatus and works associated with such a pipe or system. The definition was widened by s 25 of the Oil and Gas (Enterprise) Act 1982 to include 'any apparatus for treating or cooling any thing which is to flow through, or through part of, the pipe or system'.

A works authorisation for a controlled pipe-line may contain such terms as the Secretary of State thinks appropriate, including terms as to duration, route, things authorised to be conveyed, the persons who may be permitted to acquire an interest in the pipe-line, the methods of operation, and information to be furnished in respect of it (1975 Act, s 21(3)). Only a body corporate may be issued with an authorisation (s 21(2)).

By Sched 4, para 1, regulations are to be issued to provide for applying for a works authorisation. On an application for a works authorisation being made to him the Secretary of State may either reject it and give reasons or give notice to the applicant that it is to be considered further (Sched 4, para 2). In the latter case the Secretary of State will give to the applicant directions for advertising a notice of the application, which will allow objections to be made to the application within 28 days of the advertisement or such longer period as the Secretary of State prescribes (para 3). A map of the route will be made available for inspection (ibid). The Secretary of State may direct the serving of a copy of the advertised notice on such persons as he specifies (ibid). Where the Secretary of State forms the opinion that the route proposed for the pipe-line or part of it ought to be altered in a particular manner for any purpose mentioned in para 6 (so as to enable others to use it, for example, para 6 (*b*)) he must serve notice of his opinion on the applicant and on anyone else he considers likely to be affected by the alteration (para 4). The applicant may then claim a hearing by the Secretary of State, to influence his opinion, and others may make representations in writing and may, at the Secretary of State's discretion, be allowed a hearing (para 5). When the Secretary of State has come to a decision not to grant a works authorisation he will serve on the applicant, and on any person on whom a copy of the notice of application was served, a notice of the decision, giving reasons (except for those which in his opinion it would be against the national interest to state) (para 8). If he decides to grant an authorisation he will serve a notice of the decision on the applicant and on persons who made representations following a notice of application; and publish a copy of the notice in the London, Edinburgh and Belfast Gazettes (ibid).

It will be noted that there seems to be no provision for the holding of a public enquiry into applications for a works authorisation.

Shared use

When a controlled pipe-line has been constructed and built the Secretary of State can (subject to a right of objection of the owner of the pipe-line) require modification of the pipe-line to increase its capacity on the application of a non-owner (s 22), and he can require an owner to allow others to use the pipe-line subject to their paying for doing so (s 23). The Secretary of State may serve notice to terminate a works authorisation if the works have not been begun within three years of the authorisation (s 24(2)). If an authorisation ceases, the controlled pipe-line will vest in the Secretary of State (or the Crown Estate or Duchy of Cornwall or Lancaster in appropriate cases) (s 25(1)). By agreement it may be transferred from the Secretary of State and vest in a person who obtains a subsequent authorisation (s 25(2)).

Safety

The Secretary of State may make regulations for securing the proper construction and safe operation of pipe-lines, for preventing damage to pipe-lines and for securing the safety, health and welfare of persons engaged on pipe-line works (s 26; Submarine Pipe-lines Safety Regulations 1982 (SI No 1513) as amended by 1988 (SI No 1985); Diving Operations at Work Regulations 1981 (SI No 399)). He may appoint inspectors with powers to inspect pipe-lines and premises, vessels and installations used or intended to be used in connection with a pipe-line or proposed pipe-line (s 27; Submarine Pipe-lines (Inspectors etc) Regulations 1977 (SI No 835), as amended by the Submarine Pipe-lines Safety Regulations 1982 (SI No 1513), 1986 (SI No 1985), 1989 (SI No 1029) and the Submarine Pipe-lines (Inspectors and Safety) (Amendment) Regulations 1991 (SI No 680), 1993 (SI No 1823)). By s 21 of the Petroleum Act 1987 there is an automatic safety zone around every installation which is established for (inter alios) the exploitation or exploration in or under the shore or territorial waters or waters designated under the Continental Shelf Act 1964, s 1(7) of mineral resources, or the storage of gas or the conveyance of things by pipes. This zone is 500 metres from any part of the installation (s 21(5)). A safety zone may also be established by Ministerial order around an installation in transit to its station (s 22). Under the Offshore Installations (Safety Zones) Order 1993 (SI No 1406), in force from 1 July 1993, the safety zone provision does not apply to a vessel entering the zone in connection with laying, inspection or repair of a submarine cable or pipe-line.

Part I of the Petroleum Act 1987 contains measures for dealing with the abandonment of offshore installations.

There are more than 200 oil wells in the North Sea, with thousands of miles of pipe-lines. They must be de-commissioned and removed when the wells are dry to provide a water clearance of 55 metres; any platform in water depth of less than 75 metres must be removed entirely, (1995) *The Times*, 27 January.

Sections 34–39 of the 1975 Act, which dealt with the construction and extension of refineries under authorisation from the Secretary of State, ceased to have effect from 9 June 1987, by s 28 of the 1987 Act. An application to establish a crude oil refinery or an installation for the gasification and liquifaction of 500 tonnes or more of coal or bituminous shale per day cannot be considered for the grant of planning permission unless it is accompanied by an environmental impact assessment under the Electricity and Pipe-line Works (Assessment of Environmental Effects) Regulations 1990 (SI No 442), in force from 31 March 1990.

Offshore safety

The Offshore Safety Act 1992 was passed as a consequence of the *Cullen Report* into the Piper Alpha Disaster on 6 July 1988 when a series of explosions occurred on an oil platform (HMSO 1990, Cm 1310). Section 1 of the 1992 Act applies Pt I of the Health and Safety at Work Act 1974 for offshore purposes; it says that the purposes of the 1974 Act shall include securing the safety, health and welfare of persons on offshore installations engaged on pipe-line works; securing the safety of such installations and their proper construction and safe operation; and securing their safe dismantling and disposal. Responsibility for offshore safety was transferred administratively from the Department of the Environment to the Department of Employment from 1 April 1991. The Health and Safety Executive is empowered under s 15 of the 1974 Act to replace the large number of regulations relating to health and safety offshore. Section 4 of the 1992 Act lays down the maximum penalties which may be imposed by regulations relating to offshore safety. By s 5 the Secretary of State for Employment, after consultation, may give such directions as appear to him necessary or expedient for preserving the security of any offshore terminal or oil refinery.

Chapter 14

Telecommunications and Data Processing

By the British Telecommunications Act 1981, s 1(1), ('the 1981 Act') a public corporation called British Telecommunications (called in the Act 'the Corporation') was set up. It took over from 'the appointed day' (1 October 1981) some functions previously discharged by the Post Office. By s 10(1) before the appointed day the Post Office was to take steps to separate from the remainder of its undertaking the part concerned with the provision of telecommunication and data processing services. By s 10(2), on the appointed day all that part was transferred to the Corporation and by s 11(1) the rights and liabilities transferred included all those which by virtue of the Telegraph Acts (from 1863 to 1916, s 11(3)) were enjoyed by and incumbent upon the Post Office.

By s 2 of the Telecommunications Act 1984 ('1984 Act') the exclusive privilege of running telecommunications systems which was conferred by s 12(1) of the 1981 Act was abolished from the appointed day. A public telecommunications operator ('PTO') may run a telecommunications system if it holds a licence to do so issued by the Secretary of State or the newly-established Director General of Telecommunications ('DGT'), 1984 Act, s 7(1). The duties of the Secretary of State and the DGT include promoting the interests of consumers; promoting effective competition between persons engaged in commercial activities in connection with telecommunications in the United Kingdom; and promoting the provision of international transit services (1984 Act, s 3(2)). Other functions of the DGT include keeping under review telecommunications activities inside and outside the United Kingdom, to investigate complaints relating to telecommunications services and apparatus supplied in the United Kingdom, and to investigate conduct which may be detrimental to the interests of consumers of telecommunications services or apparatus (ss 47, 49, 50).

The Competition and Service (Utilities) Act 1992 gives effect to a government commitment contained in the Citizen's Charter (HMSO, Cm 1599) to give the Directors General for water, gas, electricity and telecommunications further legal powers to ensure that better services are provided for consumers. For each utility the Act provides for the Directors to make regulations for standards of performance, to collect information on levels of performance and make it available, to establish procedures for dealing with consumer's complaints, and to determine disputes, including those on billing. British Telecommunications was dissolved from an appointed day (s 69) and its property vested in a company nominated by the Secretary of State, British Telecommunications plc ('British Telecom').

1 Telecommunications systems

By s 4(1) of the 1984 Act 'telecommunications systems' are defined as 'systems for the conveyance through the agency of electric, magnetic, electro-magnetic, electro-chemical or electro-mechanical energy, of:

(a) speech, music and other sounds;

(b) visual images;

(c) signals serving for the impartation (whether as between persons and persons, things and things, or persons and things) of any matter otherwise than in the form of sound or visual images; and

(d) signals serving for the actuation or control of machinery or apparatus'.

By s 5 it is an offence to run a telecommunications system without a licence. By s 6(1) it is not an offence to send messages by heliograph, for example, or by any other means where 'the only agency involved is that of light' which can be 'perceived by the eye and without more'; nor is it an offence to run an apparatus on premises in single occupation or in a vehicle, vessel, aircraft or hovercraft or in two or more of those mechanically coupled together. By the 1984 Act, s 6(1), the privilege is not infringed by a broadcasting authority's transmissions.

2 Compulsory acquisition

By the 1984 Act, s 24(1) the Secretary of State may authorise a PTO to purchase compulsorily any land which is required for or in connection with the exercise of its powers or which is reasonably foreseeably required. By s 37(1) a person authorised in writing by the Secretary of State may enter upon and survey any land (if not covered by buildings or used as a garden or pleasure ground) in order to ascertain whether the land would be suitable for use for the PTO's business. Similar provisions apply to Scotland and Northern Ireland (ss 38, 39). By s 41(1) the Acquisition of Land Act 1981 applies to a compulsory purchase of land by a PTO as if the operator were a local authority. By s 40(1) for the purpose of the acquisition of land by agreement many of the provisions of the Compulsory Purchase Act 1965, Pt I apply.

By s 3(1) it is the duty of the Secretary of State and the DGT to secure that there are provided throughout the United Kingdom so far as reasonably practicable such telecommunication services as to satisfy all reasonable demands, including in particular emergency services, public call box services, directory information services, maritime services and services in rural areas.

3 The telecommunications code

Planning Policy Guidance Note 8: *Telecommunications* (1992) ('PPG 8') describes the main telecommunications systems as public communications (fixed-link through cable connections), cellular for mobile telephone users, personal communication systems (through two-way radio systems), Satellite broadcasting and terrestrial broadcasting.

Annex 3 of PPG 8 contains a summary of the key provisions contained in the Telecommunications Code in Sched 12 to the 1984 Act. The Code deals with the powers conferred on licensed operators to install telecommunications apparatus in streets and on private land. Planning and other consents are needed in addition, however.

By para 1, Sched 2 of the 1984 Act, 'telecommunications apparatus' includes any apparatus defined in s 4 above and any apparatus not so falling but designed or adapted for use in connection with the running of a telecommunications system and in particular:

> (a) any line, that is to say, any wire, cable, tube, pipe or other similar thing (including its casing or coating) which is so designed or adapted: and
> (b) any structure, pole or other thing in, on, by or from which

any telecommunications apparatus is or may be installed, supported, carried or suspended;
and reference to the installation of telecommunications apparatus shall be construed accordingly.

The Secretary of State may authorise any licensed PTO to use the Code if the operator is running a public telecommunications system or one for the benefit of the public (s 10(2)).

4 Installation

Under Sched 2 the consent of the occupier of land is needed for an operator to do works on land in connection with the installation, adjustment, or alteration of telecommunications apparatus, or to keep it installed on the land, or to enter the land to inspect, para 2(1). The owner of the freehold is bound by the agreement if he did not confer the right himself or agree in writing to its being granted, para 2(2), for as long as the occupier who granted it (not being a person with a lease of less than one year) remains the occupier. After the end of the granting occupier's term the freeholder or reversioner is not bound. Thus the operator would be well advised to obtain the consent of those with large interests in the land before investing heavily in apparatus in it. The person with an interest in possession who has not consented to the works can require the operator to restore the land to its former condition. A procedure is set out in para 21 to be followed by the person who wishes removal but the operator can serve a counter-notice and on application to a court may be allowed to retain the apparatus on the land, on terms. If the conferring of rights by the occupier reduces the value of the owner's interest in the land because of the need for the owner in due course to use the procedure in para 21 to have the apparatus removed, the owner may have compensation for depreciation of his interest and the amount is determined by the Lands Tribunal under the Land Compensation Act 1961 in default of agreement, para 4(4), (5) and (6).

5 Rights and powers of an operator

By s 50(1) of the New Roads and Street Works Act 1991 the street authority (the highway authority where the street is a maintainable highway, otherwise the street managers, s 49(1)) may grant a street works licence permitting a person or body to place or retain apparatus in the street and to inspect, maintain, adjust, repair, alter, renew, change its position or remove it. For that purpose the licence may authorise breaking up or opening the street, or any sewer, drain or tunnel under it, or tunnelling or boring under the street, s 50(1). Advance notice must be given to the street authority of intention to carry out the works, except in an emergency, ss 54(1), 52(1).

By the 1991 Act, s 129, the undertaker must reinstate the road as soon as reasonably practicable after the completion of any part of the roadworks and complete it with all reasonable dispatch. The undertaker must comply with prescribed requirements as to materials and workmanship, s 130. By s 140(1) an undertaker having apparatus in the road shall secure that it is maintained to the reasonable satisfaction of the roadworks authority and any other relevant authority as regards land, structure and apparatus of theirs. In the three years 1995 to 1998 about 60,000 miles of cable for TV are expected to be laid.

Where the operator has telecommunications apparatus installed on land, he has the right to install and keep installed lines which pass over other land in the vicinity and connect to that apparatus but they must not be less than three metres above the ground or within two metres of any building over which they pass, para 10(1). This paragraph does not authorise the installation on the land of apparatus used to support the line or any line which interferes with the carrying on of any business taking place on the land, para 10(2). The occupier may object under para 17.

By para 12 an operator has power to cross any relevant land with a line and to install the line and other telecommunications apparatus on, under or over that land and to execute works of installation and repair. The line need not take the direct or shortest route to cross the land but it must not deviate from that route by more than 400 metres, para 12(2). The operator must, except in an emergency, give the person with control of the land at least 28 days' notice of his intention to enter and do the works, para 12(4). In para 12 'relevant land' means land used wholly or mainly for a railway, canal or tramway, para 12(10).

Where any tree overhangs any street and in so doing interferes with the working of any telecommunications apparatus or will interfere with apparatus which is to be installed the operator may require the occupier of the land to lop it; the occupier may by notice object and the operator may obtain a court order for it to be lopped by the operator, para 19(5).

Where an undertaker (defined in para 23(10) as including a local authority, gas or electricity supplier or water supplier or disposer of sewage, and other bodies such as a railway, road transport or canal authority) proposes to undertake works which will or may involve a temporary or permanent alteration of any telecommunications apparatus on the undertaker's land, notice of at least ten days must be given to the operator. The operator may serve a counter-notice saying that he intends to make the alteration proposed or that the alteration must be done under his supervision, para 23(4).

The Town and Country Planning General Development Order 1988 (SI No 1813), Sched 2, Pts 23 and 24 gives permission for certain developments without the need for an express planning permission. For example, the installation of telecommunications apparatus (other than on a building or other structure) which does not exceed 15 metres in height; and in the case of apparatus on a building or other structure, an installation not exceeding the height of the highest part of the building by 10 metres in the case of a building 30 metres or more in height, is permitted, part 23. The installation of a microwave antenna is dealt with in part 24.

PPG8, which summarises the key provisions of the Town and Country Planning General Development Order 1988 (SI No 1813) in relation to relevant permitted development rights for telecommunications, states that in general it would not be appropriate for planning authorities to prohibit by art 4 directions types of development in relation to telecommunications 'unless there is serious risk to amenity', para 22. Circular 22/88 was to the same effect.

6 Compensation

Terms for compensation for installation of cables have been negotiated between the Country Landowners Association, the National Farmers' Union and various sections of the telecommunications industry. They are set out in CLA Publication W3/93 on 'Cables and Wires' and its annex on *Fibre Optic Cables on Electricity Lines*. The main sections relate to:

(1) Telephone systems operated by British Telecom, Mercury and others. In some cases the line network is hung on existing electricity (ESI) poles and annual or commuted one-off payments may be made to the landowner; in other cases lines can be laid through existing ducts or new ones constructed. New ducts will attract compensation payments.

(2) Mobile telecommunication aerials. Usually a mast of latticed steel up to a height of 35 metres is erected, with a cabin or small box at the foot, served by electric lines and protected by a secure fence. Deemed planning permission covers aerials up to 15 metres in height. Several antennae and dishes may be fixed to the mast. Average payments in the region of £2–4,500 per annum for 'tenancies' of up to 15 years are cited in the CLA Publication.

(3) Fibre Optic Cables on ESI Aparatus. Fibre optic cables can be slung along existing electricity wires, or wrapped around the earth wire or incorporated into it, with small junction boxes linking the cables. Data is transmitted along the fibre optic cables. Their use requires a further permission from the landowner and payment to him, even though the electricity wires run by virtue of an existing agreement.

(4) Cable Television. Cable networks are being installed in many urban areas, under DTI licence under the Telecommunications Act 1984. No national compensation rates have been agreed, owners should negotiate individually, using BT and Mercury rates as a guide.

Rates of compensation have been agreed with the main companies mentioned above up to 1 April 1996. They are set out in Tables given in CLA W3/1993.

In *Mercury Communications Ltd v London & India Dock Investments Ltd* [1994] 1 EGLR 229 (Mayors and City of London Court) it was held that where under para 7 of the Telecommunications Code (Sched 2 to the Telecommunications Act 1984) the county court may determine 'such terms with respect to the payment of consideration' for laying telecommunications cable ducts 'as it appears to the court to be fair and reasonable if the agreement had been given willingly', compulsory purchase principles, including the *Pointe Gourde* principle, are not applicable.

A ransom value approach, having regard to the profit which Mercury was forecasting from the use of the cables, was appropriate. Comparison of agreements with the NFU and CLA were not valuable as they related to agricultural land and did not relate to the bargaining power of the grantor. The cables were to link the Canary Wharf development with an earth station which received and transmitted international communications by means of satellite. Two agreements in 1987 and 1988 in the area had been for annual payments of £3,000. For more cable ducts, and taking inflation into account, £9,000 per annum was awarded in 1993.

Compulsory purchase principles would have given a small capital single payment. In *Alexander v United Artists* [1994] RVR 7 (CA) the plaintiff agreed to the installation of cable TV to her house and to grant the necessary wayleave. She also claimed £1.5m compensation for the installation. Held: she was not within the statutory compensation scheme and in any event had agreed to the wayleave.

Chapter 15

The Channel Tunnel

1 The Channel Tunnel Act 1987

The Channel Tunnel Act 1987 authorised the construction and operation of a railway tunnel system under the English Channel, with associated works. It provided (in the words of the preamble) for improvements in the road network in Kent which serve it and in the rail network in South Eastern England and for the incorporation of the railway tunnel system into the rail system of the United Kingdom. The tunnel was opened for public use in the summer of 1994.

Purpose

The primary purpose of the Act was to provide for the construction and operation of a rail tunnel link under the English Channel between the United Kingdom and France in accordance with a treaty signed in Canterbury on 12 February 1986 and in accordance with that to improve the road and rail network in the area with a view to accommodating the traffic (s 1). Private Concessionaires were empowered to construct and maintain the works specified in Pt I of Sched 1 to the Act, together with (in appropriate cases) Kent County Council and the British Railways Board (s 5). The land forming part of the tunnel system as far as the frontier, together with so much of the surrounding subsoil as necessary for the security of the tunnel, was incorporated into England and formed part of the district of Dover, Kent (s 10). The land comprising the seaward section of the tunnel system vested in the Secretary of State as it became occupied by the Concessionaires working from England, together with the necessary part of the surrounding subsoil (s 7).

176

Powers of acquisition

The Act authorised the Secretary of State to acquire compulsorily the land shown on the deposited plans (defined in s 49 as plans deposited in Parliament in April and July 1986) and other land to be acquired for authorised works by Kent County Council or the Railways Board (s 8). The Concessionaires, the Kent County Council and the British Railways Board might construct and maintain the works specified respectively in Pts I, II and III of Sched 1 (s 5). Planning permission was deemed to have been granted for the carrying out by the Concessionaires of 'such development as may be necessary or expedient' for carrying out the scheduled work, except to the extent that it consists of the erection of any hotel or building which is not required in connection with the movement through the tunnel of passengers or goods. There was also planning permission for the works of Kent County Council and the Railways Board (s 9). The Building Act 1984 Pt I (building regulations) and the Building Regulations 1985 (now 1991 (SI No 2768)) only applied in relation to a house or hotel as above and not to the construction of the tunnel as a whole (s 31).

The scheduled works contained in Sched 1, Pt I, included the construction of a railway and viaduct in Dover, roads in the district of Shepway and the borough of Ashford, railways in London running into Waterloo Station and associated rail works down to Ashford and Shepway.

Interference to existing works

By Pt II of Sched 2 all reasonable precautions had to be taken against interference with lines and electric wires and the Secretary of State made regulations for regulating the use of electrical energy for the operation of the authorised railway (s A). The appropriate authority could use sewers or watercourses for the discharge of any water pumped or found during the construction of the scheduled works but first needed the consent of the appropriate water authority, internal drainage board or local authority (consent not to be unreasonably withheld) (s D). There were powers for the appropriate authority to interfere with the highway for the purpose of construction or maintenance of the works authorised by the Act and to construct bridges, all in consultation with the highway authority (Pt I of Sched 7). There were similar provisions for the protection of sewers (Pt V, Sched 7), electricity undertakers (Pt VI), drainage authorities (Pt VII), and the Southern Water Authority (or its successor) (Pt VIII), the Folkestone and District Water Company (Pt IX) and telecommunications operators (Pt X). The general procedure was that the appropriate tunnelling authority deposited plans giving particulars of the intended works to the particular body and agreed them with modifications to give effect to the reasonable requirements of the particular body; the work was done causing no more disturbance than reasonable; the constructor made reasonable compensation to the bodies for loss sustained and indemnified them against claims made against them from the works; paid them any costs incurred by reason of the works (such as for altering other apparatus); restored the land as soon as practicable; and delivered to the bodies plans showing the position and level of the works carried out.

2 The Channel Tunnel Rail Link

The Channel Tunnel Rail Link Act 1995 ('the 1995 Act') authorises the construction, operation and maintenance of a Channel Tunnel Rail Link ('CTRL') between London (St Pancras) and the Channel Tunnel portal at Folkestone, Kent, with reinstatement of a disused line to provide access from the CTRL to the international station at Waterloo, London and connections to other lines. It also provides for widening the A2 trunk road and the M2 motorway.

Powers

By s 1 of the 1995 Act the 'nominated undertaker' (a person specified in an order made by the Secretary of State under s 32) may construct and maintain the works specified in Sched 1 to the Act in accordance with deposited plans. Section 4(1) authorises the Secretary of State to acquire compulsorily so much of the land shown on the plans as may be required for or in connection with the works, and by s 5(1) to acquire compulsorily land outside the relevant limits if it is required for or in connection with the authorised works, including land needed for use in mitigating the effect on the environment of any authorised works (s 5(2)). By s 5(3) this includes a right to acquire an easement or other right over land by the grant of a new right. 'Apparatus' such as a sewer, drain or tunnel may be relocated (s 5(2), (6)). All private rights of way over land held by the Secretary of State for the works shall be extinguished (s 7(1)), with an entitlement to compensation for the owner from the nominated undertaker (s 7(3)). By Sched 2, para 1 the nominated undertaker may, for the purposes of the scheduled works (amongst other things) alter the position of apparatus, including mains, sewers, drains and cables and carry out or maintain such other works of whatever description as may be necessary or expedient.

Planning permission

By s 9(1) planning permission shall be deemed to be granted for the development authorised by Pt I of the 1995 Act. It shall be a condition of the permission that work shall be begun not later than the end of 10 years from the day the Act is passed (s 10(1)).

Protection of other undertakers

Schedule 13 deals with the protection of the interests of highway and traffic authorities, of electricity, gas, water and sewerage undertakers and the National Rivers Authority (the Environment Agency after the Environment Act 1995 took effect). If the nominated undertaker requires the removal of apparatus of another undertaker, he must give not less than 28 days written notice of the requirement and afford facilities for it to be relocated by the undertaker at the expense of the nominated undertaker; the undertaker will use the relocated apparatus on terms agreed with the nominated undertaker, or decided by an arbitrator in the event of disagreement. The nominated undertaker will be liable to the highway authority, for example, for any damage caused to a highway and not made good (para 15). Works which will affect drainage work, the flow, purity or quality of water in a watercourse, cause obstruction to the free passage of fish or affect the conservation or use of water resources must be approved by the National Rivers Authority (Environment Agency).

Compensation

After the end of five years from the passing of the 1995 Act, no notice to treat shall be served and no compulsory vesting declaration shall be made, unless the Secretary of State extends the period by order in relation to any land (s 42(2)).

By Sched 4, para 8, the Compulsory Purchase Act 1965 applies to any land acquisition under the 1995 Act, with the following modifications: for s 7 of the 1965 Act there shall be substituted a provision that where a new right is created, regard shall be had not only to the extent to which the value of the land over which the right is purchased is depreciated by the acquisition but also to the damage (if any) to be sustained by the owner of the land by reason of its severance or injurious affection by the exercise of the powers conferred by statute.

By Sched 4, para 9, for s 44 of the Land Compensation Act 1973 there shall be substituted:

> 44(1). Where a right over land is purchased from any person for the purpose of works which are to be situated partly on that land and partly elsewhere, compensation for injurious affection of land retained by that person shall be assessed by reference to the whole of the works and not only the part situated on the land over which the right is exercisable.

By Sched 4, para 10, for s 58 of the 1973 Act there shall be substituted:

> 58. In determining ... whether,
> (a) a right over part of a house, building or manufactory can be taken without material detriment to the house, building or manufactory, or
> (b) a right over part of a park or garden belonging to a house can be taken without seriously affecting the amenity or convenience of the house,
> the Lands Tribunal shall take account not only of the effect of the right on the whole of the house, building or manufactory or of the house and the park or garden but also the use to be made of the rights proposed to be acquired for works or other purposes extending to other land, the effect of the whole of the works and the use to be made of the other land.

Index